ON EARTH TO MAKE THE NUMBERS UP

by
Evelyn Haythorne

Yorkshire Art Circus
1991

Published by Yorkshire Art Circus
School Lane, Glass Houghton, Castleford
West Yorkshire WF10 4QH
Telephone: (0977) 550401

© Text - Evelyn Haythorne
© Introduction - Dinah Birch
© Cover Illustration - Harry Malkin
© Cover Artwork - Tadpole Graphics
© Back Cover Photograph - reproduced with permission of The
Star, Sheffield

ISBN 0 947780 66 1
Classification: Autobiography

Printed by FM Repro Ltd., 69 Lumb Lane, Roberttown,
Liversedge, West Yorkshire.

Yorkshire Art Circus is a unique publisher. We link our books with
performances and exhibitions and offer workshops for the first
time writer. Yorkshire Art Circus projects have successfully toured
community centres, colleges, galleries, clubs, galas and art centres.
In all our work we bring new artists to new audiences.

For details of our programme of workshops and projects please
send for our brochure and book list to the address above.

Yorkshire Art Circus is a non-profit making limited company,
currently seeking charitable status.

Acknowledgements

Rachel Adam   Brian Lewis
Olive Fowler   Rachel Van Riel

**We would like to thank the following organisations for support
towards this book:**

Introduction

This is a book about the ordinary. That's what makes it so special. Writing about the years she spent growing up in Conisborough in the 1930s and 1940s, Evelyn Haythorne has nothing bizarre or exceptional to describe. Her father was a miner, and when he fell ill life became a battle for his wife and family. But then, life was a battle for just about everyone Evelyn knew as a child. Money was hard to come by, and those who couldn't help themselves could expect little from public charity. Evelyn recalls what her mother said when a neighbour was taken into the Workhouse. 'Poor old sod, they'll suck the soul out of her in there.' But the woman had been doubly unfortunate. Not only had she no money, she had no family either. And in the pit villages of South Yorkshire as Evelyn Haythorne remembers them, the family was what mattered most.

The great thought systems represented by politics and religion counted for little when times were bad. Evelyn's mother raged against the rules that had reduced her family to beggary, but could see no way to change them. Evelyn prayed to God to set things right. 'He didn't hear me.' When her brother Tom is forced to leave the house, his granny is the one who can be depended on. 'I know your gran, she'll spoil you to death!' Close, affectionate and often exasperating, family life was finally what stood between poverty and catastrophe.

Evelyn Haythorne was luckier than the old woman carried off into the Workhouse. Nothing could have sucked the soul out of her family - or, more accurately, out of her mother. Much of Evelyn's writing may be read as a celebration of the woman whose ingenuity and persistence kept her household fed and clothed in the teeth of every kind of mischance, and who taught her children, through it all, to recognise their own worth. The title of this book, like so much that happens in it, grows out of a memory of Evelyn's mother. The young Evelyn decides her best bet is to marry a rich man, to her mother's amusement: 'You'll end up like me with nowt but hard work to look forward to. Not that I'm grumbling; I'd do it all again. Sometimes I think God only put me on this earth to make the numbers up!'

Not all of this cheerful resignation, though, rubbed off on Evelyn as a growing girl, and the phrase which gives the book its title is there to be contradicted. Neither Evelyn nor her family and friends had any intention of making the numbers up. True, their grandest aspirations are constantly deflated by the life they have to lead. The book's comedy arises from Evelyn's wry memories of exalted ambitions punctured - Evelyn's first attempts at make-up scrubbed off with carbolic by an outraged brother; her cousin George's panic-stricken flight on tripping over a recumbent courting couple during his first spell of duty as a fire-watcher; her feckless neighbours having their photograph taken in a ramshackle car they didn't know how to drive.

But compassion and indignation lie beneath the laughter. Evelyn Haythorne insists that we respect the unfamous lives of her uncles, aunts, school friends, cousins, boyfriends and workmates. She also insists that we recognise each of their stories as distinct, shaped by its own particular dreams and misfortunes. It is too easy to imagine that being endlessly hard up and endlessly at work means that lives are flattened into depressed anonymity. Evelyn Haythorne reminds us how wrong we would be to suppose that.

Dinah Birch
Trinity College, Oxford.

ON EARTH TO MAKE
THE NUMBERS UP

Chapter One

"Just look at that!" Mrs Jessop said to Mother as she stood in our garden waiting to be served with some tomatoes. "It's not decent hanging her knickers on the line like that for all to see. That's if you can call them knickers; by the looks of them they're no more than two bits of lace. You won't catch me hanging out my britchers on the line, I don't believe in other men seeing what I'm wearing. Why can't she wear decent cotton drawers like the rest of us?"

"Well she won't be wearing them long, she's pregnant."

"And no wonder!"

Mam nodded towards young Mrs Jones' clothes line. Nancy Everett, now Nancy Jones, lived a few doors down and had not been married very long. "God help me if I wore anything like that. It's bad enough as it is – Bill's only got to hang his trousers up and I've got a babby!" Mrs Jessop continued, "Have you seen the way they carry on, it's not a bit like a married couple, you'd think they were still courting. He goes everywhere with her, even to do the shopping, and her hanging onto his arm as if someone was going to run away with him. He carries her bag and follows her about like Mary's little lamb. She even comes to the doorstep and kisses him in front of everybody when he's on afternoons. You mark my words she'll get that knocked out of her when she's got a house full of kids."

"Ah well, they're only young yet and have a lot to learn. I've talked quite a lot to her lately. She's alright. In fact she buys nearly all her greens here and has asked me to be with her when it's her time."

"I still say them knickers are not decent and she's asking for all she gets. I bet your husband goes red every time he sees them; I know our Bill does!"

"Don't suppose he ever notices and he's hardly likely to tell me if he does."

With that Mother moved to go inside and would have done had not the Jones' door opened and Mr Jones come out with his snap tin.

"Here just watch this." Sure enough Mr Jones kissed his wife right there on the doorstep. But he must have sensed he was being watched for he looked up and saw Mrs Jessop staring across at him. With a wave he put his snap tin down and flung both arms round his wife and gave her a big hug and a smacking great kiss. Mrs Jessop tut-tutted and turned her back on them. I stood there gazing at the offending knickers and decided I would always wear that sort when I was grown up and not the big, baggy bloomers my mother wore. I also decided I would watch Mrs Jones; especially her belly.

I'd just got ready for bed when a loud banging

came on the front door. Mother answered it and found a very agitated Mr Jones. He nearly pulled her through the door with him. "Hang on," she said, "just a minute, calm down and let me get my clean pinny on."

"What did Mrs Jones want you for last night?" I asked.

"Oh she wasn't very well. She's got a new baby girl and they are going to call it Rebecca."

"When did she get that?"

"Last night when I was round there."

"Did the nurse bring it?"

"Yes."

"Did you see it in the black bag?"

"Yes."

"Why are women always poorly when the nurse brings them a baby?"

"Well, they are not really poorly but they have to stay in bed to keep the baby warm."

"Can I see the baby?"

"Yes. If you stop asking questions and eat your breakfast I'll take you round before you go to school. I've promised I'll tidy up for her."

We went round to the Jones' and I was greatly surprised to find the baby not in bed with its mother as I'd expected but in a washing basket on a chair; it looked comfortable enough. I was disgusted, what a place to put it! I put my hand out to touch.

"Don't!" Mam warned.

I looked at the baby's screwed up face. "Hasn't it got a lot of hair?"

"Don't touch its head, it's got a soft spot and you might hurt it and don't lean over it like that, you're breathing in its face. Steady now or you'll have the basket over." All of a sudden Mrs Jones had become very bossy.

"You are a very cruel mother!" I was so angry.

"Evelyn!"

"Well, she is. She's supposed to be in bed keeping the baby warm and she's shoved it in a clothes basket."

I decided I wasn't talking to my mam when I came home at dinner time but I need not have bothered because she had no time for me, she was too busy talking to my Aunty in the living room. I sat having my dinner and I could overhear them quite plainly.

"Yes lass, it's funny now but last night was a nightmare. He was sat in the chair crying and her upstairs screaming her bloody head off and every time she had a pain she flew under the bed."

"Under the bed?"

"Yes. I'm telling you, lass, every time she had a pain, there she was under the bed and me and the midwife on our hands and knees trying to get her out. In the end I tied some rope round the door handle and said, "Here lass, swing onto this.""

"Did she have a bad time then?"

"No, lass, I've had worse but the amount of palaver she was kicking up you'd have swore we were killing her. In the end the midwife smacked her face. Well, I didn't like to see that so I came down and do you know what he was doing?"

"No, what?"

"He was on his knees praying."

"Praying?"

"Aye. Praying like mad!"

"And what did you do?"

"I told him straight. He would have been better off praying a few months ago instead of doing that what got the babby. Ooh bloody hell, I hope our Evelyn's not listening."

But I had been listening and although this may sound sneaky, I had to be sneaky to learn anything. I lived in a world of whispering and of superstition and fear; I was never allowed access to a newspaper and if I gave a second glance at my mother's weekly book, the Red Letter, I was given a back hander and the book put out of reach. Everyone around me seemed to have something to say that I was not to hear. Mam would whisper with my aunties and if she met anyone down at the shops and wanted to speak with them I was sent a couple of yards down the street out of earshot. She whispered with Mrs Jessop over the railings; the teachers whispered in the corridors and in the playground; patients whispered in the surgery and even the people behind the shop counters would lean right over and whisper to their customers. The girls in the top class would stand giggling and whispering in groups. All this caused me much annoyance and left me in a narrow, small world.

*

I had the feeling that this weekend was going to be miserable as soon as Mother opened the letter from my elder sister, Violet. I watched her as she read, waiting for the little snippets of news she usually gave me. The frown deepened on her face, "My God!" she exclaimed and jumped up from the table. The next few minutes she spent in a frenzy, rushing into the bedroom and grabbing me dad's trousers by the leg bottoms and shaking them until the few coins he had left fell out onto the floor, spinning all over the place. "Come and pick these up," she said to me roughly.

To see Mother shake Dad's trousers was nothing new. She often did it when she was short of money, justifying herself by saying that she never put her hands in his pockets. I picked up the money and handed it to her as she rummaged in the cupboard and amongst the various little jars where she kept her insurance and those other payments which she had to make weekly. She even picked our money boxes up, pushed a knife into the slot and expertly slid the coins down the knife blade and onto the table.

"Get your coat on and help Roy on with his," she said, picking Lydia up and putting her in the pram.

"Where are we going?" I asked. And what's all the rush I thought.

"Down to your Aunt Mary's," she answered sharply.

Aunt Mary lived down the bottom end of Edlington in Nelson Road and that is where Mother hurried, rushing us so fast that my legs ached and Roy had to run to keep up. Mother did not hesitate when we got there but interrupted Aunty's words of greeting.

"It's our Violet, she's been confined," Mother shrieked.

"Our Violet!" Aunty shouted back in shock and disbelief.

"Yes, our bloody Violet. I'll kill her when I get my hands on her. Will you have the kids while their dad comes home from work? And have you got owt to spare because I'm going to Manchester?"

"Steady on, lass, are you sure of what you're doing?" Aunty replied calmly.

"Sure? Of course I'm sure. I got the letter this morning which said she'd been confined but she's not said what she's got. But I'll confine her when I get there, and the woman she works for. She promised to keep a firm eye on her when I let her go and now look what's happened." Aunty just nodded and opened her purse.

"I've got two bob if that will do?"

She handed the money over to Mother who was now in such a state that she did not remember to thank her.

"I'll leave these two with you and Evelyn can come home with me to run a couple of errands while I get ready." As she turned to go out of the door she nodded to me to follow her. Once more we hurried up the streets of Edlington and back home.

It was not very often I saw my mother dressed up.

She never really went anywhere special but when she did she looked ever so posh. She had a navy blue two-piece and a shell pink blouse, high-heeled shoes and a trilby style hat with a feather in the side. But what I loved most was the fox fur with its bright, shiny eyes and bushy tail. This hung over one shoulder and fastened with a gold chain and I felt very proud to be seen with her as we walked down the main road, me on my way to Aunty Mary's and Mother to her bus.

When Dad came home we returned with him but the bungalow seemed very empty and lonely without my mother. We were used to her going out without us for an hour or two whilst she went shopping but very rarely did she leave us for the day.

I spent some of the time playing with my friends on the stretch of grass that separated the rows of identical wooden bungalows. These were mostly occupied by miners who worked at the Yorkshire Main Colliery in Edlington. My dad was a miner and so was Tom, my seventeen year old elder brother. The reason for the big gap in our ages was tht Mother had been married beforehand. Her first husband had been killed in the Great War, leaving her a widow with two children, my stepbrother and sister, Violet and Tom.

Mother arrived home very late so I did not see her until the next day. I was about to question her about Violet when my Uncle Fred came in,

"See tha back then, lass?" he enquired.

"Yes. I was back too late to come down but was coming when I'd got rid of this little lot." Mother nodded to the piles of washing sorted out into various heaps on the kitchen floor. He lowered his voice and whispered, "What's gone off then?" Mother started to laugh helplessly. "Silly bugger her. She hasn't been confined. She's been confirmed."

*

My brother, Tom, had started going out more and was taking great care over his appearance; fussing about a lot, brushing his suit and continually combing his hair. He spent an age in front of the mirror and when he was finally ready, he would look at himself before setting off. Mother obviously saw something we didn't for she would sit back and watch him then turn to my dad and give a knowing wink. One night, as he was about to go out, she said to him, "Isn't it about time you brought her home?"

Tom was a little surprised. "Who?"

"You know who I mean right enough. You can't catch old birds wi' chaff."

He grinned. "I'll ask her and see what she thinks."

"Well, from what I can make out you've been seeing her for some weeks now and it's time we saw what you've coupled up with. I reckon nowt to back street courting."

He went out saying, "All right Mam, I'll ask her."

"And you give me plenty of warning when you decide to bring her. I don't want the place looking like a tip."

The next day I heard that Tommy's 'young lady' was coming for tea the following Sunday, yet I could have sworn that the King himself was expected the way Mother carried on. Every room in the house was cleaned and its paintwork washed; fireplaces were blackleaded, clean curtains hung up and she even had me wipe the aspidistra leaves with cold milk. Not only did she bake cakes, as well as bread, but we even prepared tinned fruit and custard in addition to salmon. That Sunday afternoon we were washed and changed and Dad kept from his after club nap.

Tommy kept repeating that all this fuss wasn't necessary as she was a very nice girl who we were sure to like. Eventually, he went off to collect her and we sat, waiting impatiently for her arrival.

Lydia spotted them first and shouted "Our Tom's here with his courter!" At this Mother gave a last quick look around the room, making sure that nothing was out of place and picked up a bit of fluff that she spotted on the new coconut matting, which she had at last managed to buy from David Haigh's.

My dad stood up, looking directly through the window before saying, "Phew! Just look at this!" This was a signal, we all dived to the window but were pulled back by Mother before we reached it. Yet even a quick glance allowed me to know that I had never seen anyone as beautiful. She had long, dark, wavy hair and wore a red dress, but what really caught my eye was the high heels. Mother said later that they were Spanish heels and must have been at least three inches high. She carried a large black handbag, her lips were painted bright red and she had matching nails.

Mother gave a little sniff when she saw her but managed a smile of welcome. The girl didn't seem a bit shy as Tommy introduced her. "This is Lotty."

"My name is Loretta but Lotty is Tom's pet name for me. I've told him not to call me Lotty in front of my parents. They wouldn't like it." She spoke posh just like our teacher at school.

"Well then, we'll call you Loretta. Don't want to upset anyone. Sit down and make yourself at home." Mother nodded to a chair but the girl glanced round and moved over to the settee, pulling Tom down deside her.

She sat well back and crossed her legs, showing quite a lot of them and a good deal of lacy underskirt. Mother pointed out politely that she was showing her undies but Loretta didn't seem to hear and started chattering to my dad. All the time she was talking she kept eyeing herself through the dresser mirror.

"You don't come from round here then?" Dad asked, a lot less confident than Loretta was.

"Oh no! We come from Hampshire but my father has been transferred to Doncaster," the girl replied.

"And what does he do?" asked mother.

"He's the manager of a large furnishing store. The Doncaster branch wasn't doing very well so they sent Father to see if he could get it back on its feet."

"Oh!" said Mother, greatly impressed. "And do you work?"

"Well, at present I have a clerical job with the British Rope Works but I'm looking for something more suitable," she replied, smiling at herself in the mirror.

"Do you like living in Yorkshire then?"

"Oh, my father and I like it well enough but my mother has taken a lot of settling in. You see, she didn't want to come to Yorkshire. She has always said it's all incest and buggery up here."

Dad's mouth dropped open and Mother sat in stunned silence gaping at her.

Then she got up and started to lay the table, her lips tightly clamped together.

Lotty picked at her food daintily, still watching herself through the mirror. Much to Mother's annoyance she left some of everything on the side of her plate.

"Don't you like your food?" I asked.

"Yes. It's very nice, I'm sure, but it's good manners to leave a little of everything," she answered. That impressed me; I was very interested to know about good manners at that time. Mother looked at the wasted bread, salmon, salad and cake that was piled high on the girl's plate and then exploded.

"Who the bloody hell told you that?"

"My mother," Loretta replied. "And she should know."

"Well, it's about time she taught you right. In this house we compliment the hostess by clearing our plates; that is good manners," Mother said, banging the dish of fruit and custard in front of Tommy's Loretta. Sensing that something was wrong and not looking at the mirror, Loretta flushed and proceeded to eat every bit without answering.

At last, the meal over, Mother and I cleared the table and Loretta once more took up her position with Tommy on the settee, opening her handbag and bringing out a large bar of chocolate as she did so. She broke off a piece for me, Lydia and Roy and then began to eat it herself. Mother was so angry you could practically see her bubbling to the boil; to waste snap and then eat chocolate was adding insult to injury. Her eyes flashed. I put my piece on the end of the dresser hoping that things would cool off and I could eventually afford to eat it.

We washed up without a word, Mother banging away in the sink and Loretta looking on. We kept the clean dishes in the top cupboard in the living room and when Mother opened its door she saw the family's three china cups and saucers. They were really pretty, with deep pink roses and gold leaves painted on them but they had never been used to my knowledge for they were Mother's pride and joy.

"What beautiful cups!" Loretta said, trying to get round her.

"Yes, aren't they? But I only use them for anyone special," Mother sweetly replied before smugly walking into the kitchen.

After they had gone, Dad sat back in his chair. "Tom's got summatt on his plate wi' that one."

"Aye, did you see she left a bloody plateful here," Mother replied. "That's middle class for you, they don't know what they do want but they've got such good manners!"

*

Uncle Fred and Dad had bought some tickets in the 1935 Irish Sweepstake and while the winning numbers were being read out on the radio they had opened the big cupboard doors and chalked them up on the inside. They would chuckle excitedly together as a number was drawn near their own, shout "That was a near one!" then bend their heads to the wireless once more, willing their numbers to come out. But they didn't.

I found all this very boring and was beginning to feel a little miserable. Roy had gone out to play with his friend, Lydia was asleep and Mother was talking to Aunty Mary in the kitchen. Whenever I went into them, Mother would say, "Go and play. You're not missing owt. Little pigs have big ears." So when Loretta walked down the garden path, looking as elegant as ever, I was glad to see her.

I always admired her hair and when I told her I

wished mine was different she put her hand under my chin, studied me for a few seconds and said, "I think a fringe would suit you Evelyn. Let's go and ask your mother if she agrees and I'll cut you one." Mother said that she did not mind and so I sat in a chair near the fireplace, an old towel around my shoulders and Loretta cut my hair.

The fringe really suited me, I could see that as, thrilled, I preened myself in front of the others. Uncle Fred, who never missed a trick, thought he would save himself a few coppers so he asked Loretta to cut his hair too. She willingly agreed and soon he was sitting in the chair having his hair cut. When she had finished she said he needed a neck shave. Dad was reluctant to leave the radio in case he missed a winning draw so Loretta offered to continue.

"Are you sure you can do it?" asked Uncle dubiously.

"Well, I have shaved three ballons at the office party at Christmas and didn't burst one!" Lotty said proudly.

"That's good enough for me. Get a razor!"

Loretta went into the bathroom and came back armed with Tommy's brush, soap and razor. She lathered Uncle's neck well and began the shave slowly. She was making a good job of it too but then Tommy came in.

"What are you doing?" he enquired. At the sound of his voice she lost her concentration and looked up. In doing so, she put the razor a little bit too high and left a small bald patch on the back of Uncle's head.

With her hand over her mouth she stared aghast at the bald patch. Tommy and I began to giggle.

"Oh! My Lord!" said Dad. Uncle glared at us and said, "What's up?" Loretta looked the other way, too embarrassed to say anything.

"Nothing Fred. We nearly got a number up then, that's all." Dad's response set Tommy and me laughing again and to make matters worse, Uncle shouted angrily to us, "I wish you two would shut up and let the lass get on wi' job. I don't want her to let that razor slip!" Loretta picked up her handbag, took out her eyebrow pencil and began to colour the bald patch in as we learned that Edlington was not to be the home of the winner of Ireland's Premier Lottery.

∗

Mother was cleaning the outside of the bedroom windows. She came hurrying down and said to my dad, "Aye, aye! The bad penny's turned up again!"

"Who's that?" Dad asked.

"Your Fred! Strolling down the field as though he'd all the time in the world. Bet he wants summatt!"

Uncle Fred came down the garden path grinning like a Cheshire cat and with him the thinnest, scrawniest dog I'd ever seen.

"What's that?" Mother asked, pointing to the dog.

"Good dog is this, going to win me a great deal of money!" Uncle answered proudly. Mother and Dad looked at each other then down at the sickly-looking dog.

"Looks as if it could do wi' a good feed!" Mother sniffed.

"Ah well, that's where you're wrong. This dog only gets the best. I don't want him to get over fat 'cos he's in training. Trains on port wine and eggs he does. Yes, only the best for him."

"Well, he's not coming in here. I don't know what he'll do on my rugs," Mother snapped.

"Oh Jim's alright. He's fully house trained," uncle replied hastily.

"House trained for your house perhaps. Not for mine."

"Well, let Evelyn take him for a walk on the green until you're ready to go," Mother said in a tone that implied "You won't be stopping long Fred."

I took the lead and walked with him onto the green. The dog didn't pull me and I was quite enjoying being out with him when some boys approached us. One of them said, "God! Isn't it thin?"

"Want to gi' that dog summatt to ate, its ribs are coming through its sides!" said another. I tried to explain he was a racing dog but couldn't make myself heard with their hoots and jeers so I quickly took Jim home.

Not daring to take the dog into the house so soon after leaving, I put him into the greenhouse and went into the living-room where Dad and Uncle were discussing dog racing. I was told that Mother had gone shopping so I went back to the greenhouse where I found the dog was panting very hard. I decided to give him a drink but remembered the dog's diet of port and eggs and slipped into the pantry, reached to the top shelf and took down half a bottle of red wine. Picking up a dish I cracked two eggs into it and poured in all the wine. Then I took it to Jim who lapped it up greedily. The greenhouse was very hot and stuffy inside and for some reason Jim had got the hiccups. I watched fascinated for a few minutes but on opening the door to take him out, found that every time he stood up his back legs buckled and he couldn't walk properly. Each time I gave him a jerk with his lead he managed to stagger to his feet, then he swayed and rolled over onto the tomato plants.

Eventually, with difficulty, I managed with much pulling and tugging to get him through the door so that he just lay in a heap on the ground. Then I ran into the house and told Uncle that his dog was poorly. He and Dad rushed out and on hearing Uncle's voice, the dog tried to stand up. Uncle stood scratching his head, "If I didn't know better, I'd swear the bloody dog was drunk!"

*

When Tom was on afternoons Lotty would come on a Friday night, sleeping with me in my bed and going home the next day. This cheered Tom up no end and sometimes he would give me a Friday Penny. One Friday, however, it was getting late and Lotty hadn't arrived. Mother said that she probably wasn't coming this week and started to prepare Tommy's supper. This was a job she had been teaching Lotty to do, telling her, "There won't be money for fancy snap if you marry our Tom so you might as well learn how to cook the cheapest meat. Second steak is every bit as good as best steak if you know how to cook it right!"

I was allowed to stay up until nine o'clock on Fridays as mother said I was older than the other two and ought to be treated a little differently. She could not afford to do it with presents so she did it in the little ways she knew would please me. I felt very important when Lydia and Roy had to have their bath and went to bed early.

My dad was in the bathroom, next to the kitchen, getting a shave, Mother was peeling the potatoes for Tommy's supper and I was reading in the living room when I heard running footsteps come down the path and someone sobbing. Then the back door flew open and Lotty almost fell in; her coat sleeve torn and almost hanging off, her face deathly white. The handbag she clutched was wide open and she had also lost the heel off her shoe.

"What on earth's going off?" Mother exclaimed.

"It's a man! It's a man!" was all Lotty could gasp.

Dad did not hesitate. He ran out, stripped to the waist, his face still covered with shaving lather and ran up the garden path to see if he could see anyone as Mother sat the near-fainting Lotty in a chair.

"Get the red wine and a glass. Move girl!" Mother said sharply to me. I hurried and did what I was asked. Mother poured out a large drink and gave it to Lotty as Dad came in.

"I can't see anyone. Shall I fetch the doctor?"

Lotty started to cry and refused to have him. She sat near the big fire shivering, her head bent, her face in her hands.

Mother sat quietly watching her, then she noticed me and I was sent off to bed. I didn't want to go, I wanted to know what had really happened and what Tom would say when he came in. Mother said that he would kill him if he found out who the man was. So I walked slowly through the passage to the bottom of the stairs and stood straining my ears to listen. I heard Lotty say, "He didn't get anything, I fought him off."

"Are you sure?" asked Mother.

"Yes, I've just told you I fought him off. I kicked him and hit him with my handbag. In fact, it's broke the clasp and I've lost my purse and make-up out of it."

She then proceeded to tell Mother about it but Mother must have known that I was listening because the middle door opened sharply and she lunged at me, chasing me up the stairs. I lay awake for a long time and heard a lot of shouting and crying when Tommy came home but eventually sleep overtook me and I didn't hear Lotty come to bed.

The next morning I awoke and looked at Lotty who was still sleeping. She seemed alright but her eyes were puffed and she sobbed gently in her sleep. As I dressed I must have disturbed her for she opened her eyes and turned to me. As she did so, I noticed a lot of her hair on the pillow. Sitting up she looked at the hair as if in a stupor, trying to fathom out where it had come from. Then she reached up to her head and pulled away her hand. It was full of hair. With the same stupefied look on her face, she gazed at it and then as realisation dawned, began pulling at it frantically with both hands. "My hair!" she screamed. She became hysterical, all the time pulling and tugging at her hair, letting it drop by the handful onto the counterpane.

Mother rushed in, followed by the family. Lotty was now writhing in anguish and trying to cover her poor head with her hands and arms. It was very frightening and I heard the breath being sucked back into Mother's throat as she saw what had happened. She quickly cleared the room but left me sitting there petrified then sat on the edge of the bed in her big white flannelette nightie and put her arms around Lotty. She cradled her head against her breast, all the time rocking her to and fro and gently hushing her; tears of pity streaming down her face. Slowly Lotty calmed down and Mother left her to go into her own room to get dressed, saying "You stay with her a little while and I'll bring some tea up." Lotty sat in silence, staring at herself through the mirror which was tilted forward a little. Mother came back a few minutes later and gave us the tea. She swung the mirror upwards until all we could see was the top of the wall and ceiling. "I've sent for your parents and the doctor," she said. At this Lotty started to cry again but this time they were big, hot, silent tears.

Mother motioned me to go downstairs and with great relief I did so. I had not been down long when Lotty's parents arrived, very upset, her mother crying. The doctor came and as Lotty's mother went up the stairs with him, I overheard Mother say to Dad, "Poor little bugger, what an examination to have at her age. But at least we'll know if he did get at her." Then she saw us hovering, "You kids go out in the garden, you're not missing owt."

Lotty's dad hired a car to take her home and she sat huddled down in the back, a big scarf of my dad's wrapped around her head. Mrs Jessop saw them leave and came scurrying round.

"Is Lotty ill? I saw the doctor leave."

"You never miss owt, do you?" Mother said dryly.

"You can't help seeing through the window, can you?" Mrs Jessop answered.

"Well if you must know, Lotty's caught a nasty cold," Mother said, flashing a warning look at us.

"Oh, I thought it was more serious than that the way she was wrapped up."

"Aye, and it would be if we didn't look after her. We're not risking her getting pneumonia. No-one's neglected in this house," said Mother implying that in the Jessops' they were.

We didn't see much of Lotty after that. She wouldn't go out in the daytime and only to the pictures in the evenings; going in when the film had started and coming out before the end. After a few weeks Lotty's dad got a transfer and they moved to Dorchester. Tommy was really beartbroken but the letters got fewer for absence does not always make the heart grow fonder. Eventually we got a shapshot of her with a nice new short hairstyle; the hair shiny and thick.

Chapter Two

The Jessops moved into an empty house about two doors away from us when the old lady who lived there before and had no family was taken into the workhouse. I remember quite plainly Mother saying of her, "Poor old sod, they'll suck the soul out of her in there."

Mrs Jessop bought quite a good deal of our garden produce but was something of a nuisance because she always wanted to stand and chat. Mother didn't like these breaks in her routine but felt sorry for Mrs Jessop because she was, "As thick as a plank." Mr Jessop just had "A tile loose." Their children, two boys and a girl, were very cheeky and would not even go to the shop for their parents. Seeing this mother used to say, "Ee, I wish I could have them for a week, I'd soon straighten 'em out." The little girl, very thin and pale, with a constantly running nose, was named Joan but her family always called her Joany. She stuttered; Mother said we must not laugh at her because she couldn't help it but it was very hard not to. When she called at our house to play with Lydia, she used to stand there and say, "Is your Ly-di-di-dia coming?" until called in and given a bit of paper to "wipe the candlesticks away."

When the boys came calling they always wanted

to use our toilet until it dawned on mother that they really came to read the old comics which we used for toilet paper. As a result we began to use newspaper. We let them have the comics.

Mr Jessop had the same complaint as my Uncle Fred — he couldn't work because of his back — and therefore Mrs Jessop couldn't get up in the mornings. The school bobby was often at their house.

Joe Louis was going to defend his world title and there was a lot of talk and interest in the fight. Mr Jessop's response to this international event was to stuff a harding bag with grass and hang it with a piece of string from the clothes line. Stripped to the waist and in his pit pants — originally a pair of his wife's bloomers with the elastic taken out of the legs, all the miners wore these down the pit — he thumped away at the bag. When he hit it a little bit too hard it would swing over and over the line and then he would stop, light a cigarette and wait until Mrs Jessop unravelled it for him. He was a funny man, Mr Jessop. He once tried to ride a pig.

The Jessops once bought a ramshackle car and spent hours cleaning it. They showered it with soapy water — Mother said it would have been better used on their floors and windows — and polished the few good bits of the body until they shone. When Uncle Fred heard about the car he went out to have a look at it and was soon under the bonnet, tinkering with the engine. He was in his element, pronounced it not bad and said that he thought he could make the car go. Then, with a lot of spluttering he drove it around the square.

The Sunday following Dad was in his greenhouse when Mrs Jessop came up the garden path. "I've managed to borrow this camera from me brother," she said, "and I wondered if you could take some photographs of us all with the car?"

We all went out to watch and so did the other neighbours for it was rare to see the Jessop family dressed up and Dad with the camera in his hand. Mr Jessop sat proudly at the wheel with Mrs Jessop sitting next to him while the kids, dogs and cats piled into the back. The camera was a little Box Brownie so Dad didn't have much difficulty in using it. He took several photographs of the family inside the car, then outside the car, followed by a picture of Mrs Jessop by herself, this taken from the passenger side, and a final one of her leaning through the car window, holding the budgie cage and waving it like mad at the camera. When at last the camera ran out of film Dad handed it them back yet they still sat in the stationary car. "Well, have a good day and a safe journey." At this Mrs Jessop looked very surprised. "Oh, we aren't going anywhere. He doesn't drive!"

*

The September Leger week was the traditional treat in the area. On the day of the big race we always caught the bus into Doncaster and with Dad carrying the big shopping bag of food — we couldn't afford restaurants — we walked through the town. I loved that walk for Racecourse Road on such occasions was filled with women wearing coloured cotton frocks and men in grey flannel bags and sports coats. Big cars, with race-horse owners and bookies, tooted their horns as they weaved their way through the milling crowds; and always there was the sound of the Salvation Army bands. Standing on boxes were men dressed in colourful racing silks selling tips, each one declaring he had the winner. Two or three strong men, in next to nothing, broke out of strait-jackets and chains beside stalls selling everything from brightly dressed dolls in paper frocks to monkeys on a piece of elastic. Old men with trays slung around their necks sold bootlaces, matches and Mexican Jumping Beans, and gypsies, outside their immaculate caravans, told fortunes.

On and on it seemed to go, an ever bustling crowd; its noise filling us with excitement until at last I came to my favourite. Dressed in a bright ostrich plumed head-dress which danced in the breeze, tall, brown, wearing a red and gold tunic over a silk shirt, with a necklace of sharks' teeth, was Prince Monululu. He always smiled, had a word for all and when he spoke to me he gave me the feeling that he knew me as well as I knew him. His shout, "I've gotta horse," was the first thing you heard; you heard it before you saw him.

There were also some sorry sights; blind men and crippled singers, victims of the war. One I remember had no arms or legs. My dad always put some coppers into their tins saying, "Poor buggers, look what they've got for fighting for King and Country. Thrown on't scrap heap and begging for a living." Young as we were, we could see that it sickened him.

Nearer to the Racecourse a religious group proclaimed that The End was Nigh and that we should Prepare to Meet our Doom. I asked Dad who they were and what they meant and he told me to "Take no notice of that lot, they are just a load of conscientious objectors and not worth their salt." I didn't know what he meant but dismissed them from my mind because he had said I should. If Dad said something it was right. After all, he only wore shirt arm bands to keep the muck out of his eyes.

At last we were through the gates and onto the free course. The grass smelt good and strains of music could be heard from the fairground which followed the race meetings everywhere. When we got there the bookies had set up their blackboards and were already chalking up the odds. We would take a place against the railings and by pressing our noses between the rails we could see quite a way down the course. When the race started, however, the grown-ups took over. Then everyone pressed against us so that all I could see were the horses' legs and if I was lucky a flash of jockey silks.

I loved to hear their hoof beats and to see the clods of earth and grass fly into the air as they passed. When they had gone by, the cheering crowd would quieten down and strain their ears to listen for the loudspeaker which told them the winner. Then I would watch my dad's face anxiously and wait for the big smile which told its own story. Somehow he always managed to back the winner of the last race and with the potential winnings treat us to a couple of rides on the fair.

In between races we would sit on the grass, eat the sandwiches that Mother had made for us and watch Dad study form in the newspaper. We would also keep a look out for the man who sold William pears and Victoria plums from a tray fastened to his shoulders. I loved to bite into those pears and to feel the juice run down my chin but the thing I loved most was to suck the stone from the plum long after it was finished.

Then, after the last race was run and we had had our rides, we would walk the long road back into the town and make our way to The Red Lion in the market square. Round the back of the pub was a small yard with a couple of iron tables and wooden forms. It was a little sit down place enclosed in a stack of beer boxes. Next to the pub was a butcher's shop where Mother would buy some souse. This was pink jellied meat and very good it was too. Dad liked souse. When people called it brawn he'd always say, "That's not bloody brawn. That's souse. Brawn's brown." Mother also brought back some pigs' feet, and while she and Dad had a drink we would sit happy and contented picking the pigs' trotters.

When Dad thought that most of the crowd had gone and the bus station was nearly empty, we would go for the Edlington bus. Almost as a ritual he would then pull out a packet of Parkinson's Doncaster Butterscotch and give us each a square wrapped in its little bit of silver paper. The rest, he said, should be saved for another day.

*

A new name, Adolf Hitler, was on everyone's lips. My dad said he ruled Germany by mass hysteria and I understood that he was gathering a great army together and marching on other countries. Very soon England was talking of war.

I had heard many stories of the Great War and about the trenches in France so I was not unduly worried. I believed that the two countries at war went into a field, dug a trench and shot at each other but I soon discovered that there was more to it than that.

The Civil Defence had been formed and local people were learning how to deal with bombs and fire. I was involved and proud of my Identity Card number: KREV/280/3.

It seemed that if Edlington was to be bombed Mr Jarvis and Mr Snelson of the ARP were supposed to go into action. Mr Snelson's job was to go down the village streets in his car, blowing a whistle, and, in the event of gas being dropped, Mr Jarvis was supposed to take to his car and ring the school bell.

The first night something happened started peacefully. Most of the villagers had retired to their beds when suddenly the air raid siren sounded, throwing the village into a state of panic. We jumped out of bed, my cousin Amy went into hysterics and ran from room to room screaming and pulling at her hair and I ran downstairs, full of terror. Later I discovered that we weren't the only ones to panic for Mr Snelson not only forgot to report for duty but also forgot his car and ran around the village green in his pyjamas blowing a whistle. Mr Jarvis, on the other hand, jumped into his car and rode up and down the village's main street, window open, ringing the school bell. All this added to my terror but the quiet calm of my parents quickly soothed me and soon I was quietly playing Snap by candlelight under the stairs with Father.

The Jessops lived on one side and a man, his wife and two small boys on the other. The wife was a very timid, nervous little woman and, knowing that her husband was on the night shift, Mother had arranged that she should signal with a series of knocks on the bedroom wall if she needed anything at night or was frightened. During the air raid, when I was asleep, Mother had sent my father round to see if she was all right. We had been entrusted with a key so Father let himself in and went into the bathroom. The two little boys were crouched on the floor in gas masks, kneeling beside their mother; her hands were clasped as she prayed, tears streaming down her face. She was so badly frightened that she had wet herself several times and knelt in a large puddle. That night we added another three people into our cupboard under the stairs.

Eventually the village calmed down and went quiet. I had just got to sleep when the shriek of the siren once more wailed in the night air. This time I was really scared and I burst into my parents' bedroom. With one flying leap, I jumped into my father's bed, went straight down under the bedclothes and stuck my head up his shirt. He wondered what had hit him. Pulling his shirt up he looked down. "Are they going to kill us, Dad?" I cried. He took me into his arms and cradled my head on his shoulder. "You're all right, love, don't worry. That is the All Clear being sounded."

One night I came home from school and found the family sat around a roaring fire, a big open miners' fire. The table was set for tea and the syrup tin stood in the hearth warming so that it would be runny. I didn't have to guess what was for tea; it had to be water whelps, pieces of risen bread dough formed into balls, boiled then smothered in hot syrup. "You look half frozen, come and sit by me," Dad said, making room for me on the sofa. I sat down, thankful and glad to be home for it was bitterly cold outside. I was sitting chattering to my brothers and Dad, Mother was busy in the kitchen as usual when the door opened and in came Uncle Fred.

Mother brought in a pint pot of tea and as he took it from her he looked for a space near the fire to sit down. As we were all sitting around it there wasn't any room left to put his chair so he turned to Mother and said, "If you've got some bread I'll have some toast and I'll toast it myself!" At this he whipped the toasting fork off the wall and pushed his way to the front of the fire. We had to laugh, he was so crafty, but then you had to be crafty to get near to our fire if you were last in.

After tea, Dad went out to the coal-house with Uncle and filled the bag of coal. Then we all took our places by the fire, including Uncle Fred, who didn't seem to be in any hurry to go home, and listened to Children's Hour on the radio. When it ended Uncle got out his mouth-organ and Dad went to the drawer where he kept his and joined in. Soon we were having a right old sing-song and even Mother joined in. That night the house was filled with warmth and happiness.

Suddenly I had this strange, inexplicable feeling in the pit of my stomach. I couldn't say what it was but I do know that suddenly I was filled with fear and dread. I broke out into a sweat and, feeling dizzy, I got up from my seat and went out into the back garden. Outside I turned and looked back at the lighted window. I could see quite easily into the room, see inside, see everything normal. It was the same picture I had seen many times before but now I was seeing it through some unknown fear. How long I stood there I don't know but eventually, shivering, I went back into the house. My mother looked up as I re-entered the living-room and asked, "Are you alright? Where have you been?"

"I got a bit hot so I've been to the door to cool off," I answered. I didn't want to tell her about the funny feeling I'd had, she would have thought I was stupid and since it had all seemed so real to me, I did not want to be scoffed at. As I've grown older I often wonder if it was a premonition I had that night because within a few weeks our lives had changed.

*

Although we could not afford a week's holiday, we did have a day by the sea, for Dad was a member of the Working Men's Club and he used to pay a few pence a week all the year round for excursions. The Club also sold raffle tickets and the profits from these, together with the money the men paid in, bought us our rail tickets and gave us a shilling each to spend. We also got little pink tickets which allowed us on the roundabouts for half-price. Nearly everyone in the village went on this trip because the parents with only one child paid in as much as the parents of six children.

The hustle and bustle in our house was almost unbelievable in the two or three days before the trip as Mother cleaned the house from top to bottom and nearly killed herself with housework. The big fireplaces were black-leaded and the brass fender with its long, twisted brass poker and matching tongs cleaned and rubbed until they shone. Window-sills and doorsteps were scrubbed and donkey-stoned. If Dad said anything to her she replied, "Well, I'll be out all day Saturday!"

On the Friday, the day before the trip, she would hurry down to the Maypole to buy bacon bits, cracked eggs and a bag of broken biscuits. Then she stoked up the fire and baked small bacon and egg pies and from half a stone of flour made forty or fifty bread cakes. I don't know how she managed to carry the bag for each pie had its own saucer. The bag was almost bursting but the broken biscuits always rested on top for the train journey. Dad never came with us on these trips but always saw us onto the train and waited for us to get off at the end of the day.

We could hardly contain ourselves in the week before we went and as each day passed it was struck off the calendar as gradually we approached the date outlined in black ink. I remember it as always sunny and hot on excursion days and think I must have been about twelve years old before I knew it rained in Cleethorpes.

We never had to be called early for we didn't sleep much on those Friday nights and seven o'clock saw us at the station; Lydia and me in new cotton dresses and white plimsolls and Roy in a new jersey and flannel shorts bought specially for the trip from David Haigh's Twopenny Club. We did not have a station in the village but the train stopped in the sidings at Warmsworth. A few minutes later it was filled to capacity and left a village which was now a ghost town. We loved it when the train started for we only ever rode it once a year and walked so constantly up and down the corridors that by the time we got to Cleethorpes we had practically walked it there. Every year some child got locked in the toilet. At the sight of the sea the excitement mounted as children cheered and mothers frantically drew their little ones together to pin little identification tickets to jerseys and frocks.

On arrival it was straight onto the sands and into bathing suits which we called cozzies. Mothers with large jugs of tea sat on the beach, surrounded by shopping bags and children's clothes, watching their children play and eat bacon and sand sandwiches. Eventually, we all dressed and, after stopping at the gift shops on the sea front to buy a big hat and a stick of rock, we went down to the Prom to Wonderland to ride until our little tickets were exhausted. On the way to the station we bought Dad a present; once it was a large yellow and pink ice-cream which melted on the train home.

My dad had taken ill at the pit and had to be brought home in the pit ambulance, a very old black van with dark windows and two doors at the back held closed by an ironbar. The very sight of this vehicle rumbling down the village street struck fear into the women's hearts and it was a common sight to see a woman try to run after it then break off and cry with relief when it passed her street. When it stopped all the women stood around to see who was being brought home then quietly asked if help was needed. If the man was dead then the wife received offers of help to lay him out. Most women had a complete laying-out set of clothes ready and waiting in a drawer or trunk, the cloth kept fresh-smelling with little bags of lavender. The laying-out clothes consisted of two white cotton sheets, a flannel shirt and a long pair of hand-made white woollen socks, together with a bottle of Eau de Cologne. The cologne was used to sprinkle around the body on the three days before the burial; it helped, they said, to keep the stench of death out of the laying-out room.

After a few days, however, Dad rallied from his illness and got up again. Yet although he looked much like his old self he wasn't the same. He had always been kind and gentle and had often played with us but now the least little thing seemed to annoy him. He couldn't stand our noise and didn't seem interested in anything we had to say; he was bad tempered with Mother and she couldn't do anything right for him. I began to dread going home from school because the house seemed so miserable. Mother went around the house tight-lipped, looking poorly, and we hardly dared speak let alone laugh in case he would get upset.

One day I decided I'd had enough and voiced my feelings to Mother. "Doesn't my dad love us any more? He's always shouting at us. It's not nice living here now. I think I'll go and live with our

Violet!" Mother looked at me anxiously and said, "Of course your dad loves you. Don't you ever think otherwise. It's only because he's not very well."

"I know, Mam, but I've had a cold and so have the rest of us but we didn't carry off like he's doing. It's just as if he doesn't want us anymore."

"Now you're talking silly. Your dad loves us all as much as he ever did. You'll just have to put up with him a bit longer. He'll be better soon, you wait and see."

"Well, can I go and live with Violet then until he gets better?"

"No! You can't!" she snapped. I could feel the temper rising inside me as I snapped back.

"I'm going to run away then. I'm not stopping here with him!"

Mother was startled by this outburst; she was used to Lydia giving a bit of lip but I was usually more placid and didn't often answer back. She moved nearer to me and I backed away on my guard, expecting a clip around the ear for being cheeky. She didn't hit me though. Instead she put her head on my shoulder and said, "You poor little sod! I've been lying but I think you're old enough to understand the truth. Your dad didn't have a cold that day; he's had a heart attack and people who have these attacks are usually pretty grim to live with at first. They can't help it and we must try to understand that it is part of his illness. We must also try and be patient. He loves you, believe me. I hope you can understand what I'm saying. Things will soon be alright, just give him a little time and in the meantime I'll have a word with him. I'm sure he doesn't know how unhappy you are; even I didn't realise."

I felt a lot better, even though I didn't realise the enormity of my father's illness, and promised myself that I would try not to do anything to upset either Mother or Father. Whether or not she had the talk with him I don't know but things seemed a little better for a few days, until one dinner-time that is.

Ours was a very big table, filling most of the room and when we were all in for a meal together we could not get all the chairs in; consequently, Mother used to pull up the big chair of the three piece suite and Roy and I used to sit on an arm each with our legs resting inward on the seat. On this particular day we had got into a rather heated argument and Mother put our dinner in front of us telling us to stop arguing. Neither of us took any notice but Dad was getting annoyed. Without notice he bent down, grabbed hold of the bottom of the chair and tipped it up sending Roy and me into a huddle on the floor, the plate of dinner on top of us. Mother, who was just coming into the room with his dinner and happened to see what he had done, did not bat an eyelid but lifted his plate up and hit him squarely on the top of his head with it. He looked so funny sitting there with bits of potato and meat stuck to the hair and gravy running down his face that I wanted to laugh but daren't. All of a sudden Mother burst into tears, "I'm sorry but I've got to the end of my tether. I just can't take any more!" With this she dropped to her knees and began to cry. Seeing Mother cry made the laughter I had felt erupting inside me disappear and I too began to cry. There we all were, Dad included, on our knees in front of Mother crying our eyes out.

No-one heard Uncle Fred come in and it wasn't until he spoke that we realised he was there. "Bloody hell," he said. "What's going off here? It's like walking into a wake!" We all stood up except Mother, who was still on her knees sobbing. "Oh Fred! I nearly killed him!" Fred looked around at the broken plate on the floor and then at my dad, who still had a lot of dinner on his head, before saying with a cheeky grin, "Well, lass, if you're going to batter anything, do it to a fish!" Dad laughed, Mother laughed, we all laughed but it was more from hysterics than from anything else. "Come on kids, help me to clear this little lot up!" and turning to Mother he added, "Thee sit yourself down and I'll brew up. Thee as well!" he said motioning to Dad. Like two children they both did as they were told.

In the kitchen Uncle swung the door closed behind us and spoke gravely, "Now listen here. What's gone off here today hasn't to be talked about outside. It's family business and nowt to do with anyone else. If you love your Mam and Dad you'll button your lips and say nowt."

The recovery was short-lived and after a few

weeks, at the suggestion of the doctor, Uncle Fred and our Tom helped to bring the bed downstairs into the living room, putting it along the back wall well away from the door and possible draughts. On Dad's good days he was able to sit in an armchair next to his bed. Then he took a great interest in our comings and goings, listening intently to us and smoothing out our little problems, helping me with homework I was doing prior to the eleven plus examination. On other days he would lie, drawn and white, looking dreadfully ill and propped up with pillows. We never knew from one day to the next just what we were coming home to; we were very happy for him on his good days and miserable and worried on the bad ones. We tried to keep the house as quiet as possible and if the weather was fine we played out for hours on end, taking our meals on the lawn in what Mother called picnics.

But as the weeks went by money became a problem again and nearly everything Mother and Dad owned – my watch, her two cherished cut glass vases, and Mother's fox fur – was pawned. Any fears of being seen going to the pawnshop were ignored for Mother was now well into a battle for survival. Proud, with head held high she would walk down the main road with her bag, a regular customer, and with conviction go straight through the front entrance. It was her firm belief that this was better than crying poverty and asking help from anyone.

One afternoon I was sitting on the back doorstep

eating my bread and lard, when the Jessops' eldest boy came round. On seeing me he said, "Eh up, lard head! If the sun shines on thee tha'll make a right pot of dripping." At that moment Mother came to the back door, overheard his remark and gave him a clip around the ears. The lad burst into tears but stood his ground. "It's true. Me Mam says you feed your kids on waggon fat."

"She did, did she? We'll see about that!" With this she bounced round to the Jessops. On seeing Mother's agitated face, Mrs Jessop came to the door to meet her but she wasn't given time to speak.

"What's this you've been saying about me. I've a good mind to knock your bloody head off!"

Mrs Jessop stepped back, half afraid, as Mother strode towards her and shook her fist close to her face.

"Ooh Mam! Take your glasses off before she knocks them off!" cried Sidney Jessop, showing his delight at the prospect of a fight. But the unexpected happened; the angry flashing eyes were gone, Mother burst into tears. The worry of Dad's illness and all the starving to keep us fed properly were too much. Sidney's cruel words had been the last straw and her burden became too much for her. Sobs shook her body as the sympathetic Mrs Jessop took hold of her arm and steered Mother into their house.

After that our picnics in the garden were stopped and Mother insisted we eat in the kitchen. "No need to fill neighbours' eyes and ears up and don't go complaining to your dad, there's no reason for him to be worried."

Tommy and Uncle Fred worked hard in the garden but neither of them had Dad's green fingers and, of course, there wasn't the money for the loads of manure which Dad used to buy from the nearby farms. Consequently, they didn't get as much out of the garden and we lost a lot of trade.

The new doctor in Edlington was young and had bought the old doctor's practice. Immediately he and Dad struck up such a good doctor/patient relationship that he called in each day after his rounds to drink tea from one of the best three china cups.

He was a smart young man and wore an almost round trilby with a narrow brim, quite unlike my father's wide-brimmed nick hat. Dad dubbed him, much to his amusement, "Little Tommy round hat".

That year the blackcurrant bushes were heavy with fruit and ripe for jam making. Mother was busy with this particular chore when the doctor came.

"Mmm, that smells good!" he said.

"Aye, you can't beat a bit of home-made jam," Mother answered, spooning the jam into the clean, warm jars. When it was time for the doctor to go Mother offered him one of the jars, "I thought you might like this to finish your tea off with."

"Now that's very good of you and I'm obliged but this won't be going on any bread in our house."

"And what do you propose doing with it then?"

"Oh don't get me wrong, I didn't mean to offend, but a little of this will go into a glass and be topped up with hot water. Nothing finer than blackcurrants, they are full of Vitamin C."

Mother beamed with pleasure at this and every visitor we had for weeks afterwards had to listen to the story of how highly the doctor regarded her jam and how he used it for medicine.

Chapter Three

Everyone had to take a small mirror with them to the elocution lessons at school. This we propped up on our desks and repeated vowels, slowly watching the image of our lips. I pulled my mouth into all kinds of shapes until Mother saw me and cracked me on the back of the head saying, "Talk properly when you speak to me and stop pulling your mouth around like a duck's arse." When I went to the butcher's to get a quarter of belly pork for Tommy's supper I announced to the full shop that I required "a quarter of a pound of stomach pork."

The day I learned that I had passed my eleven plus exam and gained a place at the Grammar School was one of the most exciting days of my life. I was very proud and fully expected my parents to be so too but then the bombshell dropped. Instead of the pleasure I had expected from my mother she started to cry. "I'm sorry love, but you can't go. There isn't any way that I can afford your uniform."

"But Mam! You buy my gymslips for the school I go to now."

"Yes, I know love, but I can buy them anywhere and go to the cheapest shop for them, but David Haigh's doesn't sell the Grammar School kit, you can only buy them from Blake's in Doncaster and because they have a monopoly on them, they're very expensive." My dreams began to fade.

"But Mam, I've got to go!"

"Look! Let the matter drop. I've told you no and I've told you why; that's the end of it!" She was angry and frustrated at not being able to fulfil my dream.

"Can't we get some help for her somewhere?" asked Dad.

"If you think I'm going begging to give her high falutin ways you're wrong and anyway what sort of life do you think she'd have at her posh school if they knew we had to beg for her to get there? No! It's not as though it was one of the lads that had passed. She's a lass and she'd no sooner get through school than she'd be getting married; then where's her education gone, down the bloody washtub with the mucky nappies. Leave well alone!"

With a heavy heart I confided to my teacher. She felt very sorry for me and even went to see my parents but Mother was adamant and refused to discuss the matter any further. I couldn't help but feel that if I had been a boy a little more effort would have been made.

I decided that the only thing I was destined for was to marry and rear a family. Not knowing any other way of life I resigned myself to that fact and decided then and there I would marry a rich man. When I mentioned this to my mother she laughed and said, "Eeh lass, you've got big ideas, but you'll soon learn that rich men don't bother with the likes of us. You'll end up like me with nowt but hard work to look forward to. Not that I'm grumbling; I'd do it all again. Sometimes I think God only put me on this earth to make the numbers up!''

Still a little resentful, I went back to school but because of my disappointment my work deteriorated and I was often in trouble during sewing, knitting and cookery lessons. I was not interested in any lesson that dealt with housewifery.

When my yearly report arrived for my parents to read, Mother was angry and it saddened my dad, but, at least, he discussed it with me. ''Look love, I know you've had a disappointment but then that's life and you've got to face up to it. It doesn't matter how mundane a job is, if it's worth doing it's worth doing properly. When you grow up and meet the man in your life that you want to marry, you'll think you're the happiest, luckiest person on earth.''

It didn't seem much of a comfort at the time, but I have often thought back on his words and realised just how true they were.

''It's no good you'll have to go to the Parish,'' Uncle Fred was speaking to Mother in the kitchen.

''Fred, I can't. You know it means I'll have to send Tommy away from home. If I don't they'll make him keep us.''

''I'm willing to do that, Mam,'' Tommy interrupted.

''I know you are, son, but it wouldn't be enough.

It would be a struggle for you, even if you were married with only a wife to keep, never mind with a family. You're only a filler yet and your wage is nowt like a collier's. What happens when coal is hard and you can't fill your tubs? Your money's down as it is, lad. Lately you've had more bad weeks than good ones."

"Where will I go then?" Tommy asked plaintively.

"Nowhere in Edlington, that's for sure. They'd soon find thee," Uncle Fred interrupted.

"Talk about keeping bloody folk down. A man works nearly all his life down that stinking black hole, provides for his family and tries to keep his head above water, asks no bugger for owt and then when he's bad, he's forced to send his sons away and hide them like bloody criminals! God Almighty! There ought to be a better bloody system than this!"

Mother was really angry and indignant now. Uncle Fred nodded sympathetically, knowing what she was going through, then after a few minutes he spoke. "Well, lass, I can't see any other way out for you. You've nowt left to pawn. I know you've tried harder than most to keep the lad at home but it's no good asking for miracles; they don't happen to the likes of us. Let him go and live with his granny in Conisbrough, at least you'll know where he is and that he's being well looked after. After all, he'll be able to come and see you when it's dark."

"And how's he going to get to pit from Conisbrough?"

"Well I've got an old bike in my shed. I'll do it up and it'll look good as new when I've finished," suggested Uncle.

"It's a long way for the lad to travel from Conisbrough to Edlington and back every day," Mother protested.

"Oh come on! He's a man now, not a weakling. If he comes across brickyard he'll do it in no time."

"You wouldn't do it if it was on your bloody doorstep, so don't try shoving him away!" She stopped suddenly and lowering her voice said, "I'm sorry, Fred. I shouldn't have said that. I know you're only trying to help."

"It's alright. I know how upset you are and it's better for you to take it out on me than on the poor sod laid in room. Anyway, you always did have too much of that which the cat licks its arse with!"

Mother ignored the crude remark and in despair looked at Tom, but what could she do?

"Well, Tom lad, it's up to you. I can't tell one of my kids to go. I can't turn thee out just like that!"

She slumped into a chair, head in hands. Tommy dropped onto his knees beside her and putting his arms around her shoulders whispered hoarsely, "Don't cry, Mam. I'll come and see you every week. I know it's not your's or Dad's fault I have to go. I'll be alright with my gran." The tears filled his eyes and she kissed him gently on the cheek saying, "I know your gran, she'll spoil you to death!"

With his few possessions packed in a small suitcase and with a promise from Mother that she would keep his room ready and waiting for him, Tommy left. Dad took his departure the worst and cried bitterly for he blamed himself. I couldn't bear to watch this heartbreak and went upstairs to Tommy's room. There I knelt at the side of his bed and prayed to God to put things right for us. He didn't hear me.

Accompanied by my uncle as far as the door of the village hall Mother went to face the Parish Board but came home fuming with temper. Uncle, Dad and I listened as she repeated her story. Apparently, they had asked to see our Rent Book. "This fat ugly bugger said I'd not paid our rent for two weeks. I told him straight that I'd got nowt to pay it with and if I had I wouldn't have been there in the first place. I pointed out that if he took a good look at my book he'd see the rent had been paid on the dot for years!"

"Don't get uppity with me, woman!" he had said. This upset Mother further. Normally she would not have allowed anyone to talk to her in that way but this time she had to keep her patience.

"I'm not getting uppity at all, I'm just telling you straight."

"Ooh! You got off on the wrong foot there," Uncle said.

"I know but the silly bugger ought to have known that if I'd got the rent money I wouldn't have gone to them in the first place!"

"What happened then?" queried Dad.

"Well, they took down my particulars and said

they'd send someone round to see me tomorrow. They also asked if I had anyone in the house working. I told them no but they knew I had a son so I told them I didn't know where Tommy was and that I hadn't seen him for months. I'd better warn the children not to say anything."

"You know, lass, I've been thinking. If those on the Board say they are coming tomorrow, it's more than likely that they'll turn up today. If you've owt left in the pantry get shut of it and I'll take the wireless down home with me or they'll make you sell it," Uncle said, going to pick up Mother's radio.

"Hold it! You're not taking that wireless anywhere. I wouldn't sleep at night knowing you're capable of stripping the innards out of it the minute you got it home. No! I'll take it next door where I know it'll be safe."

She turned to us children then and said, "Now listen to me you three. If anyone asks you about our Tom you must tell them you don't know where he is. Even if it's your teacher or the vicar, say nothing. I know I'm asking you to lie but what's needful is not sinful. If you do tell then Tommy will be in big trouble, but not one half of the trouble that you'll be in!" We all gave our solemn promise as Mother picked up the radio and took it next door along with some bottled fruit and the rest of the homemade jam.

We were playing in the garden with the Jessop children when two men walked down the garden path towards us. I immediately recognised them from Mother's description. They were the men from the Parish. "Don't mention our Tom to them!" I whispered.

"Do you know Thomas Hill?" the big man asked. I felt the blood rush to my face.

"N-n-No!" I stammered.

"Are you sure? He's not in any trouble or anything. He's just a friend of mine and I'd like to know where he lives." The man seemed so nice and friendly that I very nearly confided in him, but the Jessop's boy interrupted quickly saying, "No! There's no Tommy Hill around here. In fact, the only Hills I know of are them there!" He pointed to the slag heaps that could be seen at the bottom of Back Lane. At this the fat man grunted and motioned to his companion to follow him to the back door. Mother answered and asked them in and I gave them enough time to walk into the living room, then, tiptoeing through the kitchen, I moved as near to the door as I dared. Mother would have half-killed me if she had known but I wanted to know what was being said. I could hear the big man questioning my parents.

"How long has he been ill?"

"Several weeks," Mother replied.

"What's his complaint?"

"Heart trouble, but that don't make him deaf and dumb!"

"I beg your pardon!"

"Sorry, but I thought you were under the impression that he was a half-wit or summatt!"

Mother said angrily. All the questions had been addressed to her; they had totally ignored my father.

"What are your finances?"

"Nil."

"Look missis! You're not being very co-operative, are you?"

"Look Mister! Ask a stupid question. If I had any finances I wouldn't need to ask for any," Mother replied, trying to keep control.

For the first time, the younger man spoke. "You have a nice big garden. It looks very well tended and my word, what a lot of stuff growing. Maybe you have someone who looks after it for you?"

"No! Me and the children weed it but next year when it wants turning over again I don't know what I'll do. It's too heavy a job for us."

The man nodded as though in agreement then said, "May we look round?"

"You can, but you won't find owt of any worth. Everything's gone to the pawnshop."

They wandered aimlessly around the room, then one of them said, "That greenhouse should fetch a good price. Can't you sell it?" He looked at his companion for approval.

"Yes, I could, but then I would have to buy tomatoes and marrows that I now manage to grow myself!"

"Come, come woman!" the fat man sneered. "One can live without tomatoes and marrows. You know you people are all alike. You come to us for relief and expect it on a platter. You don't even try to help yourself!"

My mother drew herself up to her full height, looked him straight in the eye and said, "Look lad! Thee keep thi relief and I'll keep mi greenhouse. I won't wish you good-day but the quicker you're on the other side of that back door the better!"

The man's jaw sagged, never had he encountered anything like this before and his dignity was injured. He was used to people grovelling to him and he began to bluster, "Come, come woman! I will not be spoken to in this manner. I am here to help the likes of you." That did it.

"The likes of us!" Mother yelled, "I'll give you the likes of us!" and at this she lost control completely. I flew out into the garden to fetch Mrs Jessop, afraid of what Mother might do but bumped into the doctor coming through the gate. I ran to him and garbled out some of what was going on inside and he ran with me into the house.

Mother had got a heavy, glass ash tray in her hand and it looked as if neither of the men dare pass her. The big man was thumping the table with his fist, his face red with anger and the young man was trying to calm him down. "I'll see you all in the workhouse before you get any help from me!" he shouted as we entered the room.

The doctor took in the situation at one glance and strode over to Dad, who groaned and fell back weakly onto his pillows; the excitement had been too much for him.

"Mr Yates! How dare you come here upsetting my patient! Get out at once or by heaven I'll make it hot for you. Go on, get out! I'll tell you all you need to know about this man later!" The doctor held the living room door open to let the men pass through. Yates ran out of the room mumbling, "It was her fault."

The doctor followed them through to the kitchen and didn't see me behind him. "My God! Can't you see that this man is living on borrowed time? There's no hope for him, he's dying!"

On hearing the doctor's words, the whole of my stomach rose up and I thought I was going to choke. In a haze I saw my mother coming towards me down the passage and I tried to grab hold of her. Frantically, I pushed my arms out towards her but they would not reach. The whole house rocked and swayed as in a distant darkness I heard myself screaming, "It's not true," and Mother's voice saying, "It's alright love, I've got you." A searing pain in my nostrils hit my brain making me cough and splutter. I opened my eyes to find the doctor and Mother bent over me. In the doctor's hand was Mother's bright green smelling salts. Helping me to my feet they began to guide me towards the stairs, but I shook my head. My first impulse was to run to my dad and love him better, like I did when Lydia was hurt, but in the same instance I felt a rush of resentment. I resented the fact that he was going to die and leave us; I resented the very tears I wanted to shed and I didn't know what to do or what to say.

I felt cold and numb and looked at the doctor half hoping I had not heard right but found only sympathy and concern on his face, not hope, as I forced my way to the door. "I'm going to the greenhouse."

I cannot remember actually walking outside but I eventually found myself on my dad's stool amongst the plants. How long I sat there I don't know, but eventually the doctor came and gave me something in a glass. "I'm sorry, Evelyn. I did not want you to find out this way; neither did your mother. I cannot tell you how deeply sorry I am."

"When will he die?" I asked.

"I cannot tell you that, love, it could be weeks or even months."

"But he is going to, isn't he?" It was important that I got confirmation.

"Yes, love, he is, and there's nothing in this world I can do to stop it happening. But there is something you can do for your mother. How old are you?"

"Eleven," I replied.

"Then you must be big enough and strong enough to help your mother through it. She needs someone and I think that someone is you!"

If my mother harboured any thought that she would get preferential treatment from the Parish because of our situation she was sadly mistaken. Mr Yates played cat and mouse with her for weeks, not making any attempt to hide his dislike of her. He could not, and would not, forgive her for the outburst and she was as bad, not hiding her contempt for the "Overriding bully who lived in a large house in Old Edlington, drove a car and had the gall to think everyone in the village was beneath him." If Mother said it once she said it a hundred times, "God help that lass of Clarke's who works up at his house. I wouldn't let a dog of mine work for him!"

The morning that Mother had to go and see the Parish Board to see if they were going to allow us any help, Dad was sleeping, so she took me with her. We entered the village hall, knocked on the door of the side room, which served as an office, waited until a voice inside called, "Wait!" and then sat down in the main hall and waited.

It must have been only ten minutes or so that we were there but to me it seemed an eternity. The hall was already filling with people, all of them plainly worried and most of them scared.

At last a man with a balding head came to the door, said, "First!" and motioned to us to follow him. A large table dominated the room and sitting at it were four men and a woman. Mr Yates sat at the head. He glanced across at us and then carried on reading the papers in front of him. No-one spoke, not even to ask Mother to sit down on one of the many canvas chairs that were stacked neatly in a corner of the room. Apart from the woman, who eyed us curiously, no-one appeared to notice our presence. The silence was overbearing, heavy, and broken only by the rustle of the papers in Mr Yates' hands. I began to feel embarrassed and kept shifting my weight from one leg to the other, while Mother stood with her back to the door, her face tightening, her wrinkles disappearing. She was getting angry and I began to wish that I hadn't come.

At last Mr Yates looked up to say "Come nearer to the desk if you don't want me to shout to you!" Mother moved nearer to the table, proud and silent. I caught hold of her hand and went with her.

"Was it necessary to bring the child?"

Mother did not answer him; she just fixed him with a cold, defiant glare.

"Oh well! Please yourself!" Mr Yates replied as he leaned forward onto his elbows.

"We have considered your case, taken into consideration that you are in arrears with your rent but after putting that straight for you, we have decided to give you a Five Shilling Food Voucher. This must be spent at the Co-operative and you will not be allowed to buy anything other than food with it. Come back next week and we will review your case further." The bald headed man offered her the voucher. Mother took it.

"Thank you!"

Back home in her kitchen she wept. "Five bob! How am I going to keep five of us on five bob? I wonder who gets the Co-op divi on that?" Having got this out of her system she put the kettle on and made some tea — tea was the remedy for everything that happened whether it be sorry, sad, happy or exciting — and then went into the living room to see if Dad was alright.

There she helped him into his chair and covered his legs with a blanket for he wanted to sit out of bed for a bit.

"How did you get on then?" he asked.

"Oh, alright. They gave me a food voucher until the big nobs at the top review our case," she said without a trace of concern. She spoke tenderly to him these days, treating him like she treated us when we were ill; her whole attitude towards him, one of gentleness and kindness.

"Will you be alright? Evelyn will stop and keep you company and get you anything you need."

"Yes, I'll be fine and it'll give us a chance to have a chat. She doesn't seem to have much time for her old dad this last couple of days." I felt my face flush at this remark because I knew that he had spoken the truth. I had endeavoured not to be alone with him since learning the truth about his condition. It wasn't that I didn't want to be with him, I did, for I loved him dearly, but just that I didn't know how to talk to him any longer. My heart was so full that tears constantly threatened, life seemed so much to bear and I felt that I could not talk about little, everyday things. I wanted to know if he knew he was going to die and if he knew what was going to happen to him after death; about what he thought of heaven, to know if he was frightened of dying. I was desperate to learn all of these things which I knew I could not ask. I had always gone to Dad with my problems but this time it could not be.

After Mother had gone to the shops I sat on the

settee keenly eyeing him. Apart from his pale face and thin body he looked pretty much the same as he always had. I had the wild hope that the doctor could have been wrong. We chatted about school and my friends but I felt uneasy. I so wanted to sit on his knee and have him hold me like he used to do. At last he spoke, "Anything troubling you?"

"No Dad! I was just remembering our dog, Bruce, that died."

"Yes, he was a nice dog. But I'm surprised you remembered him." I spluttered out my next question.

"Do you think he went to heaven?"

"Oh yes! I should think he's very happy now, probably with some old farmer to look after him."

"But he did bite the postman. Do you think he might have gone to hell?"

"No! God forgives everyone if they ask him to and are truly repentant. After the punishment old Bruce went through from your mother he was truly repentant."

"But is there a hell?" I was persistent.

"I don't really believe there is. You know, I think people make their own hell on earth," he answered.

"That true?" I asked.

"Cross my heart on it!" he said and smiled.

Mother came in very excited her eyes sparkling. "Guess what I'm going to do? I've had a brilliant idea. I saw a notice in the Fish Shop window saying they were to close for three weeks. They're having the old coal-fired pans taken out and new gas ones installed and they're also extending the shop."

"Yes, but what is all the excitement for?" Dad asked.

"I'm coming to that, if you'll give me time. You see, when I saw the notice I remembered the long queues on Friday and Saturday nights. Judging by the size of them I don't think anyone in Edlington cooks their own supper any more. I have oceans of flour and lard in stock so I spent five bob on stewing meat and dried peas and I'm going to sell pie and peas from the house!"

"You're what?"

"That's right! Selling pie and peas from the house. If there's one thing I'm good at it's pastry and once they've tried them they'll keep coming back for more!" Mother could be very confident at times.

At this she walked over to the dresser drawer and took out a pen and ink and on a large piece of paper wrote: "Home made pies and peas, Friday and Saturday nights. Orders taken through the day. All meat used is fresh." This she signed with her name and address.

The following morning was Friday and mother was up early getting the ovens ready and scrubbing the big copper out ready for the bowls of peas which she had soaked the night before. All day long she baked and the house reeked of boiling peas. Soon every available space was filled with meat pies. I looked at them and was a little apprehensive because I knew for certain that if she didn't sell we would have to eat them. Shortly after tea, however, to my amazement and delight, several people came down the path carrying basins containing notes stating their orders. My mother and I stayed up very late that night, because most of the people wanted their supper after the pubs had turned out, but when the last pie had gone it was a delighted Mother who sat counting her profits. "I'll go to the butcher's again in the morning and get some more meat. I've done a lot better than I even dared to hope!"

The next day we had a repeat performance of Friday. Mother sold out once more and had an order book filled for the following week. She had turned her five bob into nearly three pounds but the elation did not last long. On the Monday morning Mr Clark, the young man who had visited us earlier with Mr Yates, came to the door.

"Come in!" Mother said to him as she answered his knock.

"No, no! I'm perfectly alright here. I have a message for you. It has been reported to the Board that you have been running a business on Parish funds and therefore we wish you to attend the Board this morning."

"Oh aye! And who's been opening their gob then?" she asked.

"That's not for me to say." With this he nodded his head and made a hasty retreat down the garden path. Mother was fuming and wishing she could get her hands on whoever had reported her. I could see why Mr Clark wouldn't come in.

That afternoon we returned to the village hall to confront Mr Yates. When he wanted to know how much profit she made she pointed out to him that she had obeyed his orders and had bought only food with the voucher. What she did with the food, she said, was none of his business. They really had a go at each other. After she had thrown the rent money, plus the five shillings at him the bald-headed man intervened.

"I don't think we need this lady's money," he said. "In fact if everyone was as hard working and used their initiative as she had, we wouldn't have as many people on the Parish relief. I think she needs to be encouraged. Of course, we can't give her any money next week as she can now pay her own rent but I do think she should have another five shilling voucher." Mr Yates was very angry at this and tried to make him and the other members of the Board, who had nodded their heads in agreement, change their minds but he was out-voted. Mother walked out of the room as though she was walking on air. She was victorious, later admitting to the childish urge to stick her tongue out at him.

But Mr Yates was not beaten and the following week Mother received a letter from the owner of the house we rented stating that he would not allow her to use his house as a place of business and that her private enterprise had to stop.

*

After Christmas my dad took ill again and once more he spent half the time in bed. He didn't know us and would often be delirious. During the Great War he had been torpedoed three times and in his delirium would relive those nightmares.

One evening in March I came home from school, to be met in the kitchen by my mother. "Listen love," she said, "I want to tell you something before Roy and Lydia come in. You've known about your dad for a long time now and I'm afraid it's going to happen today. I want you to be very brave and to keep the children out of the house as much as possible. I've sent for Tommy and he'll help a bit." I was upset and could only nod my head to show that I understood what she was telling me.

When Lydia and Roy came home from school I asked them to play at house with me in the now empty greenhouse. I took out lots of jam sandwiches and listened to their laughter but my heart was breaking. I was twelve years old and felt weary and worn out like an old woman.

That evening my dad seemed to rally a little and, although he looked dreadfully ill, he managed to talk to us and asked that we stay in the room with him. Once more I reacted, sure that he would not die, certain that my mother had been wrong. When she decided it was bedtime we were washed, undressed and then went into the room again to kiss him goodnight. He kissed us all and when it came to my turn he put up his hand weakly and gently stroked my face. I saw the tears in his eyes as I kissed him once more, then I turned and slowly climbed the stairs.

Roy and Lydia went to sleep almost straightaway but I couldn't. I lay there silently, listening for any movement from downstairs. Suddenly I heard Mother cry out. I jumped out of the bed and descended the stairs two at a time but I was too late. He had gone, leaving Mother still holding him in her arms, tears falling onto his face.

Numb and dry-eyed I gazed at the scene. "Come on little one, this is no place for you." It was Uncle Fred who lifted me.

"Don't make me go away. Let me stay here!" I begged. But he paid no heed and carried me into the kitchen where he took out a small bottle of whisky from his pocket and, pouring some into a cup, offered it to me.

"I can't take intoxicating liquor!" the Rechabite in me mumbled. It sounded so silly that I had to fight the compulsion to laugh for I knew that it would not be laughter that came from my throat but the screams which I could feel building up inside me.

Managing to compose myself I was sitting on the pegged rug near the hearth when Mrs Jessop came in, followed by Tommy, "My poor lamb, what are you going to do now? Oh! You poor fatherless mite!" She was the type of woman who spoke in words she had read somewhere.

"They'll be looked after perfectly well, Mrs Jessop. I'm home now and I'll take care of them."

Tommy said it quietly but meant "We don't want you interfering."

Mother entered the kitchen just then and sat down saying, "He's at peace now, no more suffering for him, thank God!" Her eyes were dry now but she looked pale and spent.

"Aye, at peace now," echoed Mrs Jessop, picking up the cup I had left untouched and draining the whisky from it. "Come with me Evelyn, we'll go down to the village and get Mrs Baxter to come and lay your dad out!" she said.

"No-one is going to lay my man out except me!" Mother interrupted.

Mrs Jessop's eyes almost left their sockets. "You! But that's not decent!"

"Don't talk to me about decency. I've done everything for that man during the past few weeks, and without Mrs Baxter's help, and I'm laying him out now. Evelyn! You go to bed love. I'll look in on you soon."

My mother didn't want us children to wear black like her so she bought navy gymslips for the girls and navy blue trousers for Roy, and we each had a white shirt and black tie with navy coats and hats. The funeral was large and as we made our way slowly down the streets of Edlington, by a coincidence, a young sailor stood on the edge of the pavement and smartly saluted a dead comrade. My dad would have liked that.

At the cemetery they put the coffin down the deep hole and through tears I read the chrome plaque on the lid: Roy Manton, Aged 45 years. On top of it I threw the little posy of flowers, backed with the lacy paper serviette, which Aunty Mary made for me.

Chapter Four

The war was hotting up and the raids grew more and more numerous. After Father's death we moved house to Conisbrough. There we had an Anderson Shelter, a sort of dug-out with a roof and walls made of corrugated iron and bolted together which Grandad had covered with soil to make a lovely rock garden. Inside it was all cosy. We had a little meths stove for brewing tea, a small collapsible card table, a couple of stools and one or two wooden beer crates which we used for seats.

My mother made up some very warm siren suits with strings to pull tight at the ankles and a hood which buttoned up to the throat. She also unpicked an old fur coat for footwarmers, lined them and quilted it with feathers from an old mattress. We also kept a box of games and a small first-aid kit. At night when the sirens went we were really efficient. My grandad, a very sensible man, had drilled and rehearsed us day after day for the nights we were to spend in the shelter. At the first blast we each got out of bed, quickly put on siren suits and wellies, made our way quickly down the stairs and out through the kitchen to the back door. In the kitchen each had a parcel to collect; one had rolled-up blankets, another a basket packed with sandwiches and yet another a bucket of clean drinking water. My mother always carried a small dark brown case filled with insurance policies, birth certificates, marriage lines, one or two treasured photographs, little bits of inexpensive jewellery, her purse, needles, cotton, safety pins and anything else she thought would come in handy. This case never left her side. I used to think it was full of money because it was always kept locked and she wore the key around her neck.

The Germans were bombing Sheffield and a few miles from us a huge gun, nicknamed Big Bertha, was blasting away. When we heard aeroplanes we immediately cocked our ears and listened, waiting for Grandad to say, "It's alright, it's one of ours." I could never tell the difference but Grandad said he could. I do not know to this day whether he could or not but every time he said, "Alright, it's one of ours," we would all slump back with a sigh of relief. No-one ever questioned him.

After Dad's death Uncle Fred became more central to our life for now he had come to live with Aunty Mary, my father's sister, and their two sons, in the next street. On one wall he had a large hook, and used to sit before it for hours making nets. With a flat board and a wooden needle he wound hemp round the board, then sort of knotted it with the needle until his board was full. When he let it off there was part of the net; these nets were used to go partridge dragging. Off he would go in the middle of the night with his elder son and he would drag the net across the farmer's field. He also had an old double-barrelled gun and would buy empty cartridge cases and fill them with powder and shot. The bags he kept the powder and pellets in always fascinated me. They were bottle shaped in beautiful leather, embossed with a lovely pattern. The neck had a brass cap; when pressed with his thumb, it would give just the right amount of powder or pellet. He had always been a poacher and had been to prison for it several times. Now with the war and meat getting scarcer every day, he went out most nights. As my aunty was a partial invalid and not very strong, my mother used to do most of the cleaning and cooking. Many, many times we sat down to hares and rabbits. When it was pheasant, we always knew because the plucking was always done in the spare room and every feather put carefully in a bag and burned a little at a time. The rook pies we had had a wonderful taste.

Nothing was safe when Uncle went out poaching, not even the private fishing ponds, and many a big fat trout made its way to our table. If he went out and didn't catch anything he always seemed to meet a man who gave him a couple of chickens. When he brought his catch home for Mother to cook she always looked at him disapprovingly and made clicking sounds with her tongue. This was laughable because all the time she was tut-tutting she was skinning the rabbits or plucking the birds. He had two favourite sayings. When we were all sitting down to whatever he had brought in he would clasp his hands together, look up at the ceiling very piously and say, "God giveth and Fred taketh away," Or, with the same hand clasp, "God helps him who helps himself." Every pay day, after he eventually got work, he used to bring my aunty a bunch of flowers. This pleased her and she would carefully arrange them and stand them in a vase on top of her old treadle machine, that was until about a year later, when he was caught taking them from the flower beds in the pit yard. But, for all that, he was kind and generous. If anyone came to his home they were never turned away. I have seen him get a clean plate out and share his dinner with many a beggar; seen him break his last cigarette in two and share it with his friends, yet woe betide anyone who crossed him when he'd had a drink because he loved a good fight.

One day Aunty decided she would like her living room distempered and as wallpaper could not be bought at any price, she bought distemper. Mother and I went round to help out and in no time the walls were a horrible green. We had just finished, and mother was going to scrub the floor and put the carpets back on the bare floorboards, when Uncle, drunk as a lord was helped in by two friends. Aunty was in a rage as she told the men to drop him onto the big sofa which stood in the middle of the room and was picking his legs up to put them straight on the sofa when he opened his eyes, stared at the walls, blinked, screwed his face up and said, "Oh Lord, what am I in for this time?"

My aunty took ill after that and she could not cope, so she, uncle and my cousins moved in with us until she got better and although we were a bit pushed for room, we managed. One evening I was curled up in a chair reading my favourite comic when my elder brother came in looking very important.

"I've joined the L.D.V." he proudly announced, "and we are going to have drilling and parade at back of the British Legion on Saturday."

"What's L.D.V.?" I asked.

My cousin, who was older than me, volunteered, "Love, Duck and Vanish."

All the next week Tom strutted about like a turkey cock. He did not walk any more, he marched. He now stood at attention and saluted to himself in the kitchen mirror when he thought no-one was about. At last Saturday arrived and with much shoe shining, and nearly a week's ration of lard on his hair, off he went to his drill.

That Saturday my uncle was going down to the hardware shop for his bits and pieces, as he called them, and I asked if I could go with him. Actually I had been put up to asking him by my Aunt Mary because the shop was at the bottom of the village, past both pubs, and she knew that uncle would not let me come home by myself but would bring me back.

We went down to the shop, got what he needed and set off for home in the warm sunshine. But as we neared the British Legion we heard shouting;

Tom was doing his drill. On hearing him Uncle took hold of my hand and we nipped through the club yard and looked over the railings. Uncle said, "My God, England's last hope," and I saw what he meant, for looking through a little vent in the railings I saw rows of men, including my brother and his friends, standing like toy soldiers; their backs like ram rods, chests stuck out, heads thrown back, and with broomsticks resting on their shoulders. I could not believe it. I looked up at my uncle and whispered, "How are they going to kill the Germans with brush sticks?"

"Eh lass I don't know, probably going to 'tice them to England then batter their bloody heads in," he replied.

My cousin George, not to be outdone by my brother, decided to join the fire watchers and was thrilled when they gave him a tin hat. He went on duty with his bag slung on his shoulders, containing a flask of cocoa and a couple of sandwiches and his gas mask. His tin hat was a bit too big for him and seemed to wobble on his head as he walked. All went well with the fire watching until one night they sent him to the top of the ruined Conisbrough Castle. It was a cloudy night and although there was a moon it didn't get out much because of the moving clouds. The Castle stood in acres of ground on its own and looked very eerie in the unlit night. George did not relish this site one bit but he put on a brave face and walked steadily up to it. As he crossed the grass he stumbled over something and fell flat on his face as two undressed figures jumped up. George jumped up immediately, not knowing where to go, and shouted, "Halt, who goes there." In answer the man he'd fallen over, shouted, "Run!" And so George ran. The next day he joined the messenger boys.

Early in 1941 Aunty Mary took very ill and was taken to hospital where two days later she died. Greatly saddened by her death Mother cleaned the front room, put up trestles under the window and waited for her to arrive in the coffin which would stand there until the day of her funeral. All the curtains in the house were drawn and the house put into semi-darkness. We tiptoed around the house, spoke in whispers and Uncle Fred, very grim and white, sat in the room with Aunty Mary for hours on end.

The day of the funeral arrived and other aunts and uncles came along with cousins. I knew them all but did not see them so often so I was surprised to see my Aunt Ada's son. He was in the Army and Aunt Bessie's son was in the Navy and they were both on leave. It was a cold, rainy day and my Aunt Ada stood beside him, put her hand on Uncle Fred's shoulder and said, "Blessed be the dead that the rain rains on."

Everyone stood around crying and whispering and when the undertaker came and asked if anyone would like to see Aunty for the last time. Several of the company filed in very slowly and came out weeping. Uncle Fred was heartbroken. I can still recall his face screwed up with sorrow, the tears streaming down, his body shaken with sobs as he kept murmuring, "Oh Mary, lass", over and over again.

Despite the weather there was quite a gathering around the front gate. As we went out to get in the cabs I could not help but feel a little thrilled as I sank down in the deep soft seat. It was not often we got a ride in a car for we only used them for weddings and funerals. At last the service in the church was over and we were not long in the cemetery before the cars took us quickly back home. Two of the neighbours had stayed in the house and I was greatly relieved to find, on our return, that the curtains had been pulled back. The sun now shone on a table laid with plates of spam sandwiches, Mother's eggless sponge cakes and the big tea urn which we had borrowed from the church hall. All the men wandered off into the garden, even Uncle Fred, and were soon lighting up pipes and cigarettes. The women got their cups of tea and small plates with sandwiches and cake, and huddled round the fire in a semi-circle.

My Aunty Ada, Dad's sister, was a big fat woman with a loud voice. Although on the other side of the room, handing out sandwiches, I could hear her saying, "Wasn't it a nice service?" and "Ee, I hope I look as well as our Mary did when I'm in my coffin." I can remember thinking how stupid she was; how could anyone who had looked on Aunt Mary's poor ice cold face with its sunken eyes and grey pallor, her lips still twisted with pain, how could they say she looked well? Then I heard Aunty Ada say to Mother, "Have you any soap to spare? I need it to take into hospital with me. I go in next week."

Someone asked, "What are you going in for?"

Aunty Ada looked around the room before replying, she saw me and bent forward as did all the others. There was much whispering and I heard Aunt Bessie say, "Oh that's the big one, isn't it?"

"Yes," replied Aunt Ada looking important. "Yes, it's the big one alright," and sweeping her arm to the full extent, "taking everything away they are." All the women gathered and looked at her awestruck. "Of course, I'll be very ill for a long time after I come home," she sighed, "but that's life, one cannot do anything about it. I'll just have to manage the best I can. I've heard when they've opened you up it's a massive scar. I'll have no end of stitches." There was much tutting and shaking of heads at this. I was watching them and listening, very interested, when Mother saw me and told me to go out and play.

My friend Betty called for me just as I was leaving the house so we walked down the garden path together. "Sorry to hear about your Aunty Mary. I liked her."

"Yes, so did I," I answered, "but it's going to be worse for my Aunt Ada. Do you know, Betty, they are going to cut her open and take all her guts out. She says they are going to take everything away."

"Everything?" Betty was astonished. "You mean her liver and her kidneys?"

"Everything," I repeated. "Of course, I suppose they'll leave her heart in because if they take that she'll die."

"Yes, I suppose so," nodded Betty.

"My Aunt Bessie says Aunt Ada won't be able to have babies after it," I confided.

"Ah well, you got it wrong then," Betty said. "They aren't going to take her guts out, they are going to cut her tits off."

"How do you mean?" I said.

"Well, stands to reason, don't it. If they cut off her tits then she cannot feed babies so if she cannot feed 'em she cannot have them."

"Oh, of course," I answered. "She said she'd have a scar and would have to be stitched up." With this knowledge we walked up the street to her house.

A couple of hours later I came home to find nearly everyone had gone home except Aunt Bessie and cousin Ernest; they were staying the night. I liked the look of Ernest. He was in his teens and looked very smart in his sailor suit.

"May I touch the collar for luck?" I asked.

"Yes, of course," and then he put his hat on my head. I looked at the band around his hat; HMS Pembroke. I did not know at the time that this was a training ship.

"Have you torpedoed many Germans yet?"

He looked around him and said, "If I tell you you

must promise not to tell a soul. 'Careless talk costs lives' and come on into the garden because 'Walls have ears'." He said this very solemnly. Well, I knew this to be true because it was splashed about in every building we went into. "On my honour I won't breathe a word," I said breathlessly and followed him out into the garden.

It was growing dusk as we sat on the wooden form outside the greenhouse. He had me entranced with stories of his life at sea; of the ships he had torpedoed and the Germans he had killed. I sat there believing every word.

The next day we all went for a walk after dinner and Ernest and I walked together picking wild flowers. I think I sort of fell in love with him for he was so nice to me although I do not think for one minute that he had any kind of thoughts about me. I was a schoolgirl and he was so very grown up and handsome.

All too soon we had to go back because he and Aunty had to be on their way home. They had a long bus ride in front of them. Mother had made some tea and they were almost ready to go when I shyly asked Ernest if he would write to me from his ship. He said he would.

Aunty hugged us all, Mother hugged Ernest and we all went to the door with them. All the time I stood waiting for the bus to come I had quite unexplainable feelings inside of me and my heart lurched as, with the bus coming, Ernest bent down and suddenly kissed me. It was only a small quick kiss and I don't suppose he thought any more about it but it stunned me. I felt the blood rush to my face and my inside turned over. I managed to find a weak smile and wave as they got on. My heart was crying and I was miserable as I walked home hugging the memory of that small kiss.

For days I mooned about the place; I did not want to eat, I did not want to play; in fact I did not know what I did want. Mother thought I was sickening for something and dosed me with castor oil. Then a letter came from him with a photograph inside, a photograph to keep and cherish. There was not a lot in the letter. He told me he had arrived back at his ship, that he had enjoyed his stay and ended his letter with three crosses. I was in raptures and tore page after page of Mother's note pad up trying to perfect my letter of reply.

For a long time we kept up our correspondence and I looked forward to the postman coming but soon the letters began to come with longer intervals between them. Mother said she supposed he was out on the sea a lot and had not the time for writing but I must keep on sending mine as the lads looked forward to letters from home. Then one day I came home to find Mother crying. She had had a letter from Aunty Bessie saying Ernest had been killed at sea. I could only stare at her in shocked silence. I cannot quite remember if I said or did anything but I do remember lying on my bed and crying until there was no strength left in me. It was a very bitter blow for me and I was a long time getting over it and much too ill to go to the memorial service they had for him in his own village church.

The village was in a twitter of excitement and the streets were filled with strange faces. The chapel and the upstairs of one of the pubs was taken over by a company attached to the Green Howards. We also had quite a few Bevin Boys who had come to work down the mines and many of them obtained lodgings with the local people. I can remember one, a very shy and retiring boy who hated working down the pit. Although the couple with whom he lodged treated him like a son he was very homesick but he braved up and stuck it out. There were others, of course, who were the opposite, they thought they were God's gift to women.

Now fourteen and at my first job, working in a factory yard, I was interested in the newcomers but every time I went out, even on an errand for Mother, she would say, "Don't go near those soldiers and don't talk to those Bevin Boys. I don't want you bringing any trouble home or it's the workhouse."

"Yes, Mam," I would say, fed up to the teeth with this constant reminder.

"They'll only scarper when they'd done with you and leave you in the ditch." The ditch was my mother's way of saying pregnant.

A large complex of wooden huts arose practically overnight as accommodation for the Bevin Boys who could not get private lodgings. Known as the Bevin Huts, they had a very large recreation room in which dances were held on a Saturday night. Girls used to come from the surrounding villages to these dances, much to the annoyance of the local lads, and I saw many, many fights as girls and married women got good hidings from parents and husbands for daring to go dancing to the Bevin Huts.

I worked on the yard with my friend Betty loading up lorries and railway waggons with boxes of glass bottles. It was normally a boy's job but by now women were doing men's and boys' work. We had lots of fun. Betty and I made some new friends and soon they were asking us to join them to go dancing at the Bevin Huts. Since we both knew our parents would go berserk if we asked them if we could go alone, as they seemed to think you only went there to get raped, we talked Betty's brother into taking us. With many more lectures and reminders of my virginity Mother consented but only on condition Betty's brother kept us in sight.

We were looking forward very much indeed to our first dance. Whenever the gaffer was not looking, our new found friends taught us basic steps down in one of the big bays. The Friday before the dance was pay day so I went down to the chemist shop with my pocket money and bought some cheap face powder, a bright red lipstick, and because I had not any clothing coupons left, a bottle of liquid leg make-up. I intended looking great for this dance.

On the Saturday afternoon I got bathed using the

five inches of water only which it had been suggested was enough for wartime bathing. I had already heard on the radio that the King had ordered a black line to be painted five inches from the bottom on every bath in the Palace, although I could not think why we needed to save all this water when every day it came down out of the heavens in buckets. However, I pressed my dress, shone my shoes, stuck some of Mother's tin hair curlers in my hair and fussed about waiting in excited anticipation for the time to get ready.

I had had no experience with make-up for I had never worn any, so I slapped the powder on my face until I looked ever so pale, then I remembered someone saying that, as rouge was hard to get, women should rub some lipstick on their cheeks. I did this so liberally that I had such red cheeks that I had to put on more powder. The lipstick also presented difficulties. I pulled my mouth into all shapes, puckering my top lip until it nearly rested on my nose; trying to get a cupid's bow like a filmstar. Satisfied with my face I took out the curlers and combed my hair. It did not exactly curl for it was more like a limpy frizz but I thought it was original and very flattering. The leg make-up was more difficult. I poured it onto my hand and smeared it on my legs. It did not go on very evenly but the real trouble came when I got to my left leg for I had put so much on my right one that there was only enough to go just above my knee. I decided no-one would see as my dress covered them. I thought

"If I sit down I must remember to cross my right leg over my left." Finally I twisted, turned and went into all sort of contortions trying to draw a seam up the back of my legs but in the end I was ready and came downstairs feeling a million dollars. When I entered the living room I was greeted with a surprised gasp. Mother looked over her specs at me and half whispered, "Oh, my God!" Then she put her hand to her face and nearly had a choking fit. My younger brother hooted with laughter and pointed at me, "Look at her, she looks like a clown." I stormed out and into the kitchen where Tom was getting washed yelling, "Roy, stop that will you!"

Grabbing the towel Tom wiped his face as he turned to listen to what I was shouting, but as he lowered it his mouth dropped open and his eyes widened. "Come here and let me look at you," he said gently.

As I walked over to him his mood changed. An arm shot out like a snake striking and he grabbed me by the back of the neck and dunked my face into the water he had been using. His other hand found the soap and he started to scrub my face with it. The carbolic stung my eyes, went up my nostrils and some found its way into my mouth. I kicked and screamed. The carbolic made my eyes and my nose but, most of all, my dignity smart.

Mother heard the commotion in the kitchen, came in and made him let go of me. Now I was really mad. This was the first and only time I ever turned on Tom because since the death of my father I had clung to him. This time, however, my temper was beyond reason and it was like a mad bull that I flew at him. Arms and legs, nails and teeth, no holds were barred. Eventually Mother dragged me off, clouted my ear and pushed me onto a chair. Then the tears flowed; they came in big drops, ran down my face and some splashed onto the leg make-up leaving great white splash marks. Then everyone left the kitchen and let me cry it out. I've never been a pretty girl but now I looked positively ugly; my eyelids were swollen, the whites of my eyes were bright red and, when the tears stopped, my face was a blotchy purple. Mother came back into the kitchen and put her arms around my shoulders.

"Come on love, come and sponge your face. Wash that muck off your legs."

"I can't go now, I look a mess," I wailed. "He spoils everything and it's nowt to do with him. I'm working now not a kid."

"Alright, alright, don't start off again, but you wasn't going out looking like a painted tart," said Tom, popping his head around the kitchen door.

"I shall please myself and shan't ask you, so there," I answered.

"You just listen to me, young lady, if ever I see you painted up again I won't wash your face I'll wring your bloody neck." I knew by his tone that he meant it.

"That's enough from both of you," said Mother, busy putting cold tea into a saucer. "Sit back and I'll see if I can get a bit of the swelling down around your eyes. I'll help you to put your make-up on, though I can't understand why you should want to wear the muck in the first place." She picked up the powder and lipstick. I hadn't much faith in her, she had never used it before but I got a nice surprise when she had finished.

Chapter Five

As I grew older I recognised the way wartime placed a terrific strain on women. They fed their families on small rations, balanced clothing coupons, stood in long queues and then spent nights in the shelters worrying over their loved ones in the forces and the terror of seeing the telegram boys. Any event that eased the tension a little was grasped and enjoyed to the full so the wedding at Betty's, on a bright October morning, was a great release.

The same big luxurious cars that did the funerals came bedecked with ribbons; their seats covered with white sheets, artificial flowers and big satin bows hanging in their windows, and to me that ride in the cab to church and back was the best part of the wedding. When we arrived at church the guests were standing outside for apparently there had already been three weddings that morning and they were running late. As I stood there my mother came up to me with my old woolly cardigan and said, "Here put this on while the bride comes." I looked at her with horror; cover my dress with my cardy, never! I would stick the chattering teeth and goose pimples for the rest of the day but my dress was going to be seen by all.

I didn't have to stand too long, we had only been there a minute or so when the church doors opened and out walked the couple who preceded us and who had just been wed. Also in white the bride carried a big bouquet of flowers, yet choose how she held the flowers she could not hide the big bulge under the dress. The groom was a stranger to the village and as soon as mother clapped eyes on them she poked me in the back.

"See that's what yer get with them Bevin Boys."

"He isn't a Bevin Boy, Mam, he's an art teacher," I answered softly.

She sniffed. "Ugh, he looks as though he's taught her summatt, and made a pretty picture of her."

All the time she was saying this she was nodding her head sideways at the couple in disapproval. I was sure they would hear so with a gentle push I got her through the church door and was greatly relieved when our bride arrived.

The bride entered on the arm of her father and with Betty and me behind them, we walked solemnly down the aisle to the whoos and ahhs of the guests and arranged ourselves at the altar. Harry was petrified and did not even turn to greet his bride. The vicar, who had been at our church for many years and christened some of our mams and dads, began clearing his throat to start the ceremony. Suddenly Betty's mam ran up to Harry, lifted his coat, tugged at the back of his trousers and in a loud voice said, "Daft sod yer, you've left tickets on your suit." With this she tore them off the paper and hurried back to her place in the front pew. The vicar looked over his spectacles at the congregation and in a patient voice, said "Shall we proceed?"

Harry's mother smiled and nodded as the bride gave Betty, her chief bridesmaid, her bouquet to hold. Betty dropped it and as we both bent to pick it up we banged our heads together. Once more the vicar peered over his spectacles, once more cleared his throat and started the service. All this did not help poor Harry and by the time we got to the part where he had to repeat the service after the vicar he was in a right state. It was as though he'd got a pair of rubber lips; the words would not come out properly. He made a real mockers of it.

The vicar said, "To love and to cherish."

Harry said, "To love to cherish."

The vicar tried again, "To love and to cherish."

Harry repeated, "To love to cherish."

By now the vicar was determined that this service was going to be correct and therefore in a loud, booming voice, "To love *and* to cherish."

Suddenly the light dawned. Harry grinned sheepishly and said, as if surprised, "Oh aye, to love and to cherish."

From where I stood I heard Harry's mam say, "Stupid sod, I could go up there and smack him. He's making a right mess of it." Whether she meant Harry or the vicar was not quite clear.

At last much to everyone's relief the ceremony ended and after the signing of the register we all came out to have photographs taken. Our Lydia, now eight years old, and her best friend Beryl, had gone up the bus terminus day after day and stood hours waiting for the buses to pull in so that they could beg the conductress to empty the small, round coloured bits they had clipped off the tickets into a paper bag. Now they threw their confetti and then went round with a paper bag distributing the excess so that everyone had some to throw.

When we arrived back at Betty's home we sat down for our high tea at the trestles we had borrowed from the chapel on the wooden forms which came out of the doctor's surgery. We drank a toast to the happy couple with a thimbleful of sherry, ate the meal, cleared away and then put on the gramophone and played the records. Lydia and Beryl were taking tap dancing lessons and so two wooden baker's trays were put side by side on the floor for them to dance on. Betty and I danced in the yard with the music coming through an open window.

*

Molly Drayton worked on the same bench with me. Two months earlier she had received a letter saying her young husband was missing and this news had turned Molly from a laughing happy girl into a quiet sad-eyed woman. Her body went to skin and bone and some days she looked really haggard from sleepless nights. She had been off for a month with the shock of this news but she was now trying to pick up the threads of life again by settling back at work. We girls at first tried not to mention the war or even our boyfriends but this made conversation a bit stilted because since we were all teenagers, boys were our favourite conversation. I remember one of the girls getting engaged and proudly bringing her ring to work on Monday morning. We formed a ring around her and were all admiring it, and asking to try it on when Molly walked towards us. When she saw her the girl started to put it quickly away not wanting to upset Molly; it had not been so long before that we had all stood around her. But for all her sadness Molly went up to the girl and asked to look and smilingly tried the ring on with the rest of us as the gaffer shouted, "Do you think you're in a holiday camp? It amazes me how you lot get any bonus." His bark was worse than his bite and he was not a bad sort really.

This particular day, towards lunchtime, he came up to Molly and told Molly that her dad wanted her outside. Her face went taut and white, she looked at me for a long minute, bit her lips and followed the gaffer to the doors. From my position I could see straight through them. Molly's dad was waiting for her. "What's up?" a few of the girls said as out of curiosity they drew nearer to my bench. Our hearts were heavy for Molly because it wasn't normal practice for outsiders to come onto the yard and hardly ever near the doors, therefore I watched with great curiosity as Molly's dad took hold of her hands and spoke to her. Suddenly Molly jumped into the air, hugged her dad, hugged the gaffer and ran back into the warehouse yelling "He's alive!" Arms outstretched, tears rushing down her cheeks, she grabbed anyone who was in her path before falling into a dead faint. We all stared in hushed silence at the poor crumpled body on the floor. Then one by one we burst into tears; tears of joy for the poor lass, tears of joy for the young man who was her husband and tears of relief because we knew her father had not brought her the news we had dreaded.

Eventually they brought Molly round and the gaffer offered to run her and her father home in his car telling us before he did so that we could take an extra quarter of an hour for lunch. When the gaffer returned we learned that Molly's husband was alive and well but was in a Prisoner of War camp. We felt rather disappointed that he was not on his way home to Molly but saw that captivity was better than being dead.

Two days later, after Molly got over the shock, we clubbed together and bought her a lovely bouquet of flowers. As I lived near her I was the one chosen to deliver them. That afternoon I hurriedly got bathed, changed, had a quick tea, picked up the bouquet and set off to Molly's home. She still lived with her parents because of the housing shortage but was saving her money so that she could buy a house after the war. Molly was pleased to see me and delighted with the flowers.

I followed her into the living room to meet her mam and dad, and found there a young dark and handsome man. When Molly introduced me my heart went thud as he smiled and stood to shake my hand. I was over the moon, he had such good manners. All the boys I knew would have never stood up when they were introduced and this small action made me feel really something. I smiled back at him but to my annoyance felt myself going into a deep blush.

Soon we were chatting away like old friends. I found out that he was Molly's brother-in-law, Raymond, and that he lived in the next village. I told him about my work and family. I do not think that either of us would have noticed that it was time to go home had Molly's dad not kept yawning and winding up the alarm clock. As I made for the door, Raymond said "Wait a minute, I'll walk you to your home."

I felt a blush of pleasure at the prospect but as he moved towards me I noticed he had a bad limp. "Oh don't bother," I said. "It looks as if you can hardly walk. Have you been hurting your leg?" He turned his head away as Molly quickly said, "No, he had an accident when he was little and had to have an operation which has left him like that."

I could have bitten out my tongue as I looked at Ray standing dejectedly, his head turned away from me. 'Oh, I'm sorry."

"Don't be," he blurted out.

I began to feel really uncomfortable. "Well, in that

case now I know your leg isn't painful I'd love you to walk me home," I said. His face brightened at this. He smiled and as he bent to pick up his cardigan. Molly put her hand on my shoulder and whispered, "Good girl."

We walked home slowly. I felt as though I'd always known him for he was so easy to talk to and I was thrilled when, on reaching our gate, he asked me if I would go to the pictures with him. I went to bed that night very happy, my mind full of Raymond. I hurried home from work the next day and with mounting excitement dressed for the pictures. We met often in the next few weeks, and went for such long walks together that I hardly noticed his limp. He taught me the names of different birds, what to look for when they were flying and how to identify them high in the air. He named the ducks and geese on the ponds, identified wild flowers and made me laugh when I admitted that up to then I had thought they were weeds. He loved the outdoors and I loved being with him for he was gentle, kind and thoughtful. He did not look on the birds, rabbits and other wild animals as a form of food but saw the beauty in them and showed this beauty to me. Even now I can still thrill at the beauty of the countryside, its birds, animals, trees and plants, still marvel at nature. He taught me beauty and for three months I continued to meet him whenever possible as my life became wrapped up in him. I know I neglected Betty but she understood.

Ray's eighteenth birthday was on a Sunday. I had been saving up to buy him something nice and decided on a book with lovely illustrations of birds which described walks in Yorkshire. He was very pleased with it and took it to the pictures with him that night when we went to see a war picture about the Air Force. It interested Ray and he hardly held my hand at all on our way home but was very quiet and thoughtful. I asked him if anything was the matter but he only squeezed my arm and shook his head. I went home that night feeling restless and very puzzled. I wondered if I had said or done anything he didn't like. I questioned myself and eventually fell asleep feeling uneasy.

When I met him again the next day he was very serious. I sensed that he had something to tell me so I asked him what it was. "Yes, love, I have," he said. "You know I'm eighteen now and old enough to join up. Well I'm going to join the Air Force as a rear gunner." Almost without realising it my eyes went to his lame leg. "My leg won't stop me," he said defiantly. "I won't need it sat in the back of a plane. Anyway look at Douglas Bader he's flying them and he hasn't any legs."

"Yes, love, but he is a flyer," I answered faintly, my heart sinking at the prospect of Ray going away.

"That's what I'm saying. If he can fly without any legs then I can fire a gun in the back with a lame one." He sounded so confident that I was near to tears. "Cheer up love. I'll get plenty of leave and I'll write to you nearly every day. I must go you know.

It's right that I go now I'm of age. I want to get into the war and take an active part in it. You do understand, don't you?"

"No, I don't understand," I cried. "I don't know why you should want to leave a safe job and leave me to go shooting up some poor sods in an aeroplane."

"Well, them poor sods are shooting our poor sods up, aren't they? And we all will be poor sods if they win the war," he answered angrily.

"I don't want you to go," I said softly. "Please don't go Ray."

"I'm sorry but I want to go, love. I must go. It's something I've wanted since I left school and nothing can change my mind."

He spoke tenderly putting my head close to him and kissing me. I knew I would never be able to change his mind so I did the only possible thing and answered, "Alright, if you must." I smiled up at him and he kissed me once again.

All that evening he talked of nothing else but the Air Force. He knew as many aeroplane names as he did birds. He talked about the gun he would be using if he was on a particular plane. He knew the best place to hit an enemy aircraft to demolish it. I can remember thinking was it possible that Ray, who was so kind and gentle with animals, could without any compunction kill human beings and be so pleased at the prospect of doing so? I shivered slightly in the night air.

Ray was as thoughtful as ever. He took my shiver

as a sign of being cold and straightaway put his arm around me.

It only seemed to be a matter of days before Ray met me outside work, his face showing the excitement he was feeling. "My papers have come. I'm to go for my medical on Tuesday morning at 9.30 prompt," he said proudly.

Once more I had an awful sick feeling at the pit of my stomach and once more prayed that they wouldn't accept him. I didn't want him to go, we had been so happy, why did he want to spoil it all now? His joy was so great I could not speak my thoughts to him, I could not do anything but listen to him as he went on about the Air Force.

The night before his medical he was on top of the world, full to the brim with his plans and talked of nothing else. His enthusiasm was so great that it seemed that he believed that if he got in a plane England would have no use for another air gunner, that he could take on the whole of the Luftwaffe singlehanded. He arranged to meet me the next evening from work and the long day dragged. At the end of my shift I left quickly, running through the gates to where he would be waiting for me. He wasn't there. I looked up and down the busy street several times thinking he had not got back in time and then I made my way home wondering when I would see him.

"A young girl brought this letter for you late this afternoon," Mother said when I reached home. I slowly opened it, and read:

Dear Evelyn,

You will be pleased, I am sure, to know that I did not pass my medical. They won't accept me because of my leg. I am feeling very bitter about it and as I don't seem to be of any use to my country or the Air Force I can hardly think I will be of any use to you or any other woman, so I've decided to call off our friendship. Don't try to get in touch with me because I don't want to see you again. Thank you for the happy hours we've had together.

Ray

I sat staring in disbelief at the piece of paper. "Call off our friendship"; was that all it had meant to Ray? I had loved him so much. I looked up at my mother who was looking at me very concerned. "Why didn't you tell me you had a boyfriend?" she asked.

"You! How could I tell you anything like that. You wouldn't have understood if I'd told you. You would have only lectured me. You've never trusted me. You seem to think that all I'm going to do with boys is end up with a baby. You've never given me credit for common sense and to have you lecture me on Ray would have dirtied something that was lovely and good."

All the bitterness of Ray's letter welled up inside me and in my resentment of him I took it out on her but I stopped when I saw my mother's hurt look and rushed upstairs. I didn't cry very much, I just lay stunned and let the grief take over. She came upstairs to me but I ignored her as she sat on the bed.

"Look love, I'm sorry. I didn't realise what my nagging was doing to you. I didn't really mean it but I've never been able to talk to you properly about things. I could never bring myself to talk about it really. Of course I trust you, really I do, it's just I don't want anything to happen to you. I know now I've gone the wrong way about it but really I was only trying to warn you what can happen to a young girl."

I was startled at my mother's words because I had never known her to say that she was sorry before and I knew from her tone of voice that she really meant it. I also knew she really loved us but expected us to know that without constantly showing it. Never mushy, she did not drool over everything we did like some mothers. I sat up and looked at her. "I'm sorry for making you my whipping boy, Mam."

"That's all right, love, now tell me all about it," she answered.

I told her of my meetings with Ray, about his leg and his wanting to join up, his disappointment at not passing his medical and ended by showing the letter to her. She sat listening, not interrupting and at last said, "What are you going to do?" I shook my head. "Why not go and see him in a day or two when he's got over it? Probably you will be able to talk things over or write and invite him here. I'll make a cake and he can come to tea. I'm sure everything will turn out all right. Come on downstairs now and I'll make us a good hot cocoa and you have an early night, then you'll feel better." I had to smile. An early night was mother's remedy for nearly everything.

After two days I still did not hear from Ray so I wrote to him asking if he would see me, if not at my home then perhaps somewhere else where we could talk. My letter remained unanswered.

Chapter Six

Life for me had now become dull and boring. I seemed to spend my waking hours working or queueing for Mother. I still had not quite got over Ray but was used to being without him. Betty had got herself a boyfriend and so I often seemed to be at a loose end. I got up for work one Monday and got ready, feeling very restless. I now wanted something different in the way of work, something for the war effort, but I couldn't go into the services because I was not eighteen nor was I old enough for munition work. That Monday morning I was utterly fed up and said as much to my workmates. "We can't do anything to help the war," I complained, "only sell flaming flags." One of the girls chirped up, "Unless we join the Land Army. Have you seen their uniforms, they're ever so smart? My cousin's in them and she says it's a great life. In fact, I wouldn't mind joining them." At this, my ears pricked up and I thought, "That's for me."

During the dinner hour six of us sat around the canteen table and talked of the Land Army. One of the girls, Doreen, was not really interested but we persuaded her to join with us saying that we would ask if we could all go to the same farm or maybe split up on two farms nearby. We did nothing but talk of the Land Army all that day and at the end of it rushed home to get our parents' permission. It took me quite a while to get my mother to consent but I finally managed it and went to work the next day to find out how the others had got on. They also had gained permission so we immediately wrote off for our papers. We were ready and prepared to do our bit for England and when the papers arrived we were all twittering with excitement. We all sat once more around the canteen table and helped each other to fill in the forms. Doreen was still not sold on the idea and needed further persuasion to fill in her papers.

We had to wait several weeks before we were told to go to Doncaster to be interviewed. After that there was silence.

The weeks turned into months then one morning Doreen came into work waving a buff-coloured envelope. "Well, girls," she said, "it looks as if we've made it." Our eyes popped. "We haven't got one," we all chorused. "Well, the post hadn't been when I came out," I said. "I bet it will be there when I get home." The others agreed and once more our day was filled with nothing but Land Army talk. We did not think about hard work but about getting away from home, of being independent, and the glamour of being in uniform. To our disappointment, not one of the remaining five of us received a buff-coloured envelope. To some extent this gave us hope because, although we had not got our call-up, neither had we been refused. So day after day we waited but there was nothing.

"I wish they would hurry up and send for you," complained Doreen. "I go next Monday and it's a long way from here to Northumberland."

"Oh, it's forced to come any day now," I answered confidently but still no post came.

Eventually we went to see the gaffer and asked him if we could have half an hour off work to see Doreen off from the station. "Yes, you can go," he said grudgingly, "but I shall dock the time off at the end of the week."

We all arrived at the station where Doreen was to catch her train. She stood on the platform with her mother weeping by her side. On seeing us, the mother stopped crying for a few seconds to say, "If it weren't for these bloody idiots you wouldn't be going away." At this we all looked at each other uncomfortably because it was the truth; we had badgered Doreen into joining us when she really didn't want to. The train came and Doreen stepped onto it with her suitcase, looking lost as the guard came up the platform banging the carriage doors shut. Two big tears rolled down Doreen's cheeks and to cheer her up we sang, "Wish Me Luck As You Wave Me Goodbye" at the top of our voices until the train was out of sight. When it was no longer possible to see Doreen, her mother turned on us angrily but before she had time to say much, we hurriedly scarpered off the platform and back to work.

At seventeen I left the Glass House and went working with Betty making surgical steel blades in a steel factory in Sheffield. Although it was not the war work which we wanted, the fact that most of our surgical blades went to military hospitals, both at home and abroad, gave us a certain satisfaction. It was a long and tedious journey getting to Sheffield in those days. We had to get up very early in the morning and take the path down the steep, rocky crags to the railway station. The train was a slow one which stopped at every station between Cadeby and Sheffield. The journey used to take about an hour and a half and got us into Sheffield an hour before the time to start work. Fortunately nearby was a British Restaurant where we could buy huge mugs of steaming tea and bacon dips, thick slices of bread dipped into the hot frying fat. As neither of us had time for breakfast before setting off to work, Betty and I really used to enjoy this luxury. The winter months on that journey were agony. We went slipping and sliding down the crags, often not able to find the paths for the thick snow, and arriving at the station, often had to stand on the freezing platform waiting for a slow train which was sometimes two hours late.

*

England at this stage of the war seemed to be flooded with men with strange tongues and uniforms. We had many of our allied countries' forces in Yorkshire and also a large number of Americans. The American troops were mainly found in the cities and towns and hardly any came into the villages. Mother had her say on Americans and in a voice of doom predicted what could happen to young girls who went with the Yanks but since I hardly ever saw one, it fell on deaf ears. Yanks to me were people who introduced nylon stockings, chewing gum and a new vocabulary. No longer were we asked if we were going to the dance, it was fashionable to be asked if we were "going to cut a rug." At the Bevin Huts we were not asked to dance; instead the boys would sidle up to us and, with a mouth full of gum, jerk their heads towards the dance floor and mumble, "Come on, snake, let's rattle." The waltzes and foxtrots were forgotten as we jived in pleated skirts and matching pants. We loved the jitterbug but you had to be very fit to perform it for it was fast and furious with much shaking of the legs and arms. You were picked up by your partner, sent high into the air and swung down again to pass through his legs without touching the floor, brought back up and thrown away to land back on your feet, before getting back to the leg shaking.

The Germans were now bombing with everything they had. Our hearts went out to the people who lived in the towns and cities but apart from a few incendiary bombs which landed on Denaby pit, we lived in comparative safety. The war seemed very remote from us and only posters proclaiming "Is your Journey Really Necessary?", "V — For Victory" and asking us to use our handkerchiefs when we coughed, served as reminders. The LDV now called the Home Guard had also changed; rifles with bayonets replaced broomsticks. Volunteers now wore the thick khaki uniforms of the Army. They had also earned our respect as they became a very efficient fighting force. Every day the rumours got stronger that we would be invaded and we realised that our very lives depended on these men.

By now nearly every available woman was on munitions and women and girls who had never seen inside a factory turned out to make the badly needed ammunition. Many of the great torpedoes and shells had messages painted on them such as "To Hitler with love". Factory women, in their smart boiler suits, brought in a new fashion and we girls copied the turban, binding our hair with scarves or any bright coloured material. The munitions money was very good and helped bring in the higher standard of living which meant that "Uncle", the pawnbroker, soon went out of business. The news on the radio was also very heartening. We were steadily winning the war and everywhere people were smiling and cheerful despite the shortages and constantly rising prices. We became more and more determined and everyone now had their shoulder to some imaginary wheel. Even Mother took a job in the Glass House. She worked three shifts, mornings, afternoons and nights, on a weekly rate as a machinist. These machines stood in front of the furnaces and men stood on platforms above them filling moulds with molten glass. Mother's job was to take the red hot bottles from the moulds with clippers and put them down for another woman to pick up on a very long-handled shovel before putting them into the leer, a moving belt, which cooled them down and made them ready to be packed. The heat was intense and women could only work a quarter of an hour on the machine. After this they moved on to the leer for a quarter of an hour before taking a quarter of an hour's rest in the canteen. It was so common for women to faint in the heat that no one sympathised but just chorused, "Wheel her out and waft her." Mother, like many of the others, got some very nasty burns on her arms and legs from the red hot glass.

It was whilst I was working in Sheffield that I saw my very first homosexual man. Betty and I had gone for our tea to the British Restaurant as usual but on entering found it full apart from a table with just one man. When we entered his back was to us. We took our tea but were taken aback when he turned; he wore lipstick and long dangling earrings. "Good morning," he said in a light voice and although inside we were bursting with laughter we managed to keep pretty straightfaced and answer him although I dare not look at Betty or she me. Betty was just taking a drink from her mug when the man produced a handbag and took out his cigarettes.

The sight of the handbag did it, she choked on her tea, it came down her nose and this set me off into a fit of uncontrollable laughter. When we had calmed down we could only think that he must be an actor made up for his part from a theatre somewhere nearby because being brought up in a narrow world by our mothers we had never even heard of gay men.

That night, sitting down with the family having my meal, I began to tell them about it. Mam suddenly jumped up from the table yelling, "Oh my God, she's mixed up with bloody lesbians now. You can leave that job straightaway. I'm not having you among that lot." As I had never heard of the word lesbian before I did not know what she was ranting and raving about so I asked her what was wrong but was met with flashing eyes and an angry red face. She bent over me and with a finger pointing nearly up my nose said, "You listen and listen good. You don't have anything to do with that sort. They are sick, they are a pack of dirty buggers and no decent persons have owt to do with them." I tried very hard to explain to her that I did not know what he was but it was of no use and I escaped from the room none the wiser. Next day at work I asked a woman, who was a lot older than me, about the man. She looked a little taken aback but took me and Betty to one side and told us what he was and what he did. We were shocked and for years we thought that she had been pulling our legs. It was not until we were a lot older that we realised that she wasn't.

On Saturday nights we usually went to a dance to talk about boys and clothes. Whitsuntide was only about a month away and it was custom on Whit Sunday to have some new clothes despite the shortage and clothing coupons. The latest fashion was the two piece suit worn with a blouse and many women, whose husbands were in the forces, unpicked their suits, fashioned a skirt out of the trousers and cut down the jackets to go with the skirt. Shirts were also unpicked and altered into blouses. Demob suits became very necessary in Conisbrough. Enterprising mothers turned dark woolly blankets into very fashionable coats, with a little trimming here and fancy buttons there, and second-hand dealers did well. A new hair fashion called the Edwardian style also reached us. The hair was piled on top of our heads and clipped tight with two windsweeps at the front. As my hair was not quite long enough to go right up I got a clean stocking, tied it with a small knot and rolled my hair around it in a sort of sausage roll, known as the Victory Roll.

*

Coming home from work one evening I turned the corner in Main Street and bumped into Doreen, home on leave from the Land Army. I had to look twice before I recognised her because she wasn't at all what I expected. Before she left she was on the plain side but now she sported a bleached blonde hair-do, smart khaki knee breeches, thick stockings, a green pullover, and a narrow-brimmed hat was perched jauntily on the back of her head. The air of confidence and vitality which she displayed left me feeling very drab indeed but I liked her and therefore I ran waving and calling. Just then a young man came out of the cigarette shop and took her arm. "Hi, Doreen, how are you?"

"I'm great, Evelyn. Here, meet my new husband Joe Briggs."

It gave me quite a shock to find she was married. None of my friends knew for if they had they would have mentioned it. I saw Doreen's mother quite often but avoided her. I was at the age when I could be embarrassed and I had grown ashamed of the episode at the station when we had sung "Wish Me Luck As You Wave Me Goodbye." Now it seemed a silly thing to have done although at the time we were quite serious. Fortunately Doreen did not mention it.

I took a long look at her Mr Briggs. His brown leathery skin was so different from that of the pit lads. They were pale and sickly looking; the pit muck lying heavy on their eyelids gave the impression that they were always tired. Joe Briggs clearly worked for all his time out of doors and it was obvious that he was a farmer, but a nice friendly one who soon engaged himself in our conversation. Of course, I wanted to know about her life in the Land Army in Northumberland, about the farm she worked on, her friends and many more things but I quickly realised that she was indifferent and answered my questions very loftily indeed.

"And how's life treating you?" she asked almost condescendingly.

"Oh, pretty much the same except I work in a steel factory in Sheffield now."

"My God, I would die if I had to be cooped up all day in a factory."

"Well, someone has to do it," I said half apologetically but also going to the defensive.

"Then thank God it's not me," she said wrinkling her nose. I was now getting more than a little irritated with her attitude.

"How long are you home for?" I said changing the conversation.

"Only a couple of days and that's long enough in this dump."

Well, I didn't have much experience with the outside world, I had never been many miles away from Conisbrough but I wasn't going to let her get away with that. "There are a lot of places worse than this," I answered pointedly. "I like Conisbrough." As I spoke I found I was telling the truth; I did like it and had somehow lost my urge to leave. How dare she call it a dump! I was proud of our old church, proud that the village was mentioned in the Domesday Book, proud of the historic castle that had connections with Ivanhoe, and the beautiful surrounding countryside. I liked the long walks through woods and fields but most of all I liked its people. True, everyone knew everyone else and a secret wasn't a secret very long but I doubted if a warmer, friendlier, more helpful people could be found anywhere. I also knew, as young as I was, that Conisbrough was for me and that I would never willingly leave it.

NEW BOOKS
FROM YORKSHIRE ART CIRCUS

If you have enjoyed this book, why not get another good read from Yorkshire Art Circus? You can order our books in any bookshop or write direct to Yorkshire Art Circus, FREEPOST LS2336, Castleford, West Yorkshire WF10 4BR. Please make cheques payable to Yorkshire Art Circus Ltd. If you order one book only, please add £1.50 to cover postage and packing; if you order two or more books, postage is free. If you prefer to use an ACCESS or VISA credit card please ring 0977 603028 and we will take your order immediately. Please quote order reference EH/91.

TANGO DOWN THE CORRIDOR
Joan Gordon   **£4.99**

ISBN 0 947780 68 8

"When we came north they called my mother 'love.' She didn't like it."

Told with insight and wit, this new autobiography is a perceptive examination of the tensions which exist in a family where the mother is isolated and the father works long hours. Joan Gordon endures the schoolgirl hardships of navy bloomers knitted in four-ply, the adolescent shock of getting a bosom and the fortunes of the ballet class. Racial prejudice is never far away and the value of education for girls a subject of real debate.

Joan Gordon's first book is a wonderful evocation of the thirties as remembered by a young girl who lives her formative years in a Leeds suburb.

SAFE HOUSE
Diane Tingle   **£4.99**

ISBN 0 947780 63 7

Diane is a successful chef in a busy city restaurant, juggling the demands of work with the demands of bringing up children on her own. But within two months her confidence is shattered by violence. In this remarkable story Diane overcomes grief, fear and poverty to rebuild her sense of identity, and make a home for her family.

"Powerful stuff" Radio 4, Kaleidoscope.